A Rant on
Atheism, Credulity and Counselling
The Dangers of Faith in Therapy

By Alexander Hylton ParkerCopyright
© 2020 Alex H Parker

Visit Alex H Parker websites for more information and to get to know the author:
www.alexhparker.com
www.plackybag.co.uk
www.plesseycastle.com

Published by Plessey Castle Autodidact.

CONTENTS

"Fear is the main source of superstition, and one of the main sources of cruelty. To conquer fear is the beginning of wisdom."~ Bertrand Russell.

What's the answer to the great question of 'Life the Universe and everything?' This was the central theme at the centre of The Hitchhiker's Guide to the Galaxy.' By Douglas Adams. The answer was 42. It was a comedy answer with a point. What is the 'great question?' The Great Question to Life the Universe and Everything is not a question, it's a title. To understand the answer, we must first know what the question is. After an entertaining story, the question was found to be, *"What do you get if you multiply 6 by 9"*. The answer to this question is not 42, it's 54. The point was, 'the universe is fundamentally flawed.' Over the past century, scientists have tried to formulate a theory of everything which will combine Einstein's theory of relativity with quantum theory. Both theories are mathematically correct and testable, but follow different physical rules. It's as if the universe is fundamentally flawed. According to current physics, through the process of entropy, the universe will dissolve into nothing. On the plus side, we live for around 100 years, so we'll miss the anticlimax. In 'A Christmas Carol' Ebenezer Scrooge was given similar news by his long dead friend Jacob Marley. Scrooge asked Jacob to "Speak comfort to me." But Jacob replied "I have none to give." If this appears a little dark. I have no hope to offer. Scrooge was shown his entire life devoted to money and how no one will mourn his passing. He was shown his dismissive attitude to the love of his life who ended their relationship, and the family whom he ignored. He was also shown how he exploits his clerk with long hours and little pay which causes hunger and death for his children. The story ended with Ebenezer adopting a charitable attitude toward the suffering in his community. The story was about regret and the decision to lead a meaningful life. Scrooge's old philosophy of 'humbug,' was contempt for the community spirit of compassion, generosity of material things and personal time. In a universe of meaninglessness, the human species suffers hunger, illness and poverty and exploitation. In affluent countries we find people who suffer loneliness, mental illness and crime. Even those who appear to have everything have been known to take their own lives. I could go on listing the dark side of human existence but as Scrooge discovered, joy and meaning in life can be found. The apparent meaninglessness of the universe and the cruelty of an existence where we're condemned to appease our fears of hunger and death. People who are and have all the things needed are faced with boredom and the realisation of meaninglessness. One day, all the things we've worked so hard to acquire will be left behind.

Eric Idol said: *'Life is just a show, keep them laughing as you go. Just remember that the last laugh is on you.*

End Credits for the Movie "Life of Brian"

These words are from the film 'Life of Brian.' It was a comedy movie about a world full of injustice and the human search for salvation from reality. The message of the movie didn't offer a solution to the problems of humanity, but rather pointed out the absurdity of existence prescribing the distraction of dancing and singing to cope. I can think of worse advice. If you're standing in a line of convicted criminals, waiting to be executed by a firing squad, I'm certain you'll enjoy the experience much more if you go out singing together, 'Wish me well as you wave me goodbye" by Gracy Fields.

Woody Allen said:

"In my next life I want to live my life backwards. You start out dead and get that out of the way. Then you wake up in an old people's home feeling better every day. You get kicked out for being

too healthy, go collect your pension, and then when you start work, you get a gold watch and a party on your first day. You work for 40 years until you're young enough to enjoy your retirement. You party, drink alcohol, and are generally promiscuous, then you are ready for high school. You then go to primary school, you become a kid, you play. You have no responsibilities, you become a baby until you are born. Then spend your last 9 months floating in luxurious spa-like conditions with central heating and room service on tap, larger quarters every day and then Voila! You finish off as an orgasm!"— Woody Allen

As the title suggests, you're about to read a rant. I find it difficult to avoid the drive to shout when faced with arguments designed to seduce vulnerable people. Clever reasoning with long-winded words and a sprinkling of quotes from academia is enough to make something appear scientific.

One of the great commandments of science is: 'Mistrust arguments from authority.'~Carl Sagan.

Demon-Haunted World:p.52

Authority is a position of prominence which has an influence on people's behaviour, even though they may have no expertise in the subject. An example of this is the British Royal Family. Any opinion they express is published by the press as if it was newsworthy, and the public would use their opinions to justify their own point of view or to justify abolishing the monarchy. This is why they're encouraged to keep their opinions private. Pop stars also have an influence on the thinking of their followers through their lifestyle and song lyrics. John Lennon and Bob Marley are two musicians who are frequently quoted on social media and have value due to their notoriety rather than any great personal wisdom. Not to demean what they've said, but to show how we're influenced by the sayings of people who appear to be authorities based on success in any subject. Authority based on fame is dangerous because it can influence the direction of the world. We live in a world where democracy reveals what influences people's voting habits. In the western world, it's a consistent formula that charisma and existing fame are the path to leadership. Within 40 years, the USA had two TV stars as presidents. Ragan and Trump already had the affection of a nation, so becoming their leader wasn't a difficult endeavor. President Kennedy and Obama look like movie stars. We've always voted for the best looking prime minister in the UK. Tony Blair had no competition against the less charismatic John Major. John Major and Margaret Thatcher were never threatened by Neil Kinnock or Michael Foot. Tony Blair resigned as PM and the new leader was Gordon Brown who is extremely intelligent, but had the charisma of a baked potato. David Cameron was young and charismatic. Suitability as an authority is rarely based on experience or knowledge, rather its good looks, personality and success in any walk of life. The following quote is a paraphrase from The Buddhist teaching to the Kalamas gives the first advice against making arguments based on authority. *"Believe nothing, no matter where you read it, no matter if I have said it, unless it agrees with your own reason and common sense."~Buddha.* People are visible authorities, but something written in a book, newspaper and the internet are accepted as reliable authorities for no other reason than they're something you read. Facebook has been one of the most destructive sources of fictional news and racist propaganda.

Religion caused writing to develop to a sophisticated level. It required the conveying of concepts and abstract ideas. Hebrew, Cuneiform and hieroglyphics were all developed to record spiritual concepts and laws. These writings were read exclusively by the educated classes and revered by the masses. I don't know who the first person was who said 'You shouldn't believe everything you read.' but it's a saying I have heard all my life and with good reason. Millions read the newspapers every day, and it's well-known people accept every word they say. This has proven to be a problem for people who've been arrested for high profile murders. In Britain A professor was arrested as part of an investigation into a young woman's murder. The British press published his name and photos of him looking eccentric. They made a plea to the readers to contact them with any sensational stories about the professor which would be entertaining reading. It was later revealed he wasn't involved in the murder, but by the time he was exonerated publicly he had suffered a torrent of abuse and threats. The power of the written word carries credibility, by virtue of it being published. I was seduced by clever rhetoric to join a fundamentalist christian church when I was 21. I was of a mindset easily led by the written word. I was Convinced Astrology is a science and Uri Geller presents proof of psychic powers. I wanted to be introduced to religion with clever answers to hard questions. So I was ready to be caught by the first church to throw me the bait. But why was I desirous to be seduced by the rhetoric of religious literature?

I was never comfortable with my inevitable death. Death is the eventual end of existence. This is the devastating truth we must all face, unless you can persuade yourself you can live forever like Conor McCloud from Highlander. The reason for believing in life after death is the comfort it brings, but comfort is desirable, especially if you have a life full of suffering. Stories about life after death and reincarnation assist humans to cope with the apparent meaninglessness of existence and our cosmic insignificance. Replacing Reality with a promise is opiate like dulling the pain of a toothache. The hypnotic nature of these beliefs is effective. Prayer, religious literature and inspiring talks help communities to focus on eternal existence. Spiritual teachers offer anecdotal evidence from scholars. A professor who declares he brought a girl in Africa back to life using prayer or the Doctor who claims he experienced an out-of-body experience while dying on an operating table. Biased research distorts the facts by the power of academic credentials. Pseudo-science uses propaganda, cherry picked quotes from academics, and a rudimentary understanding of quantum mechanics to satisfy their believers. At its base, it will always have a dogmatic belief in the infallibility of a holy text. One thing a bias agenda avoids is evidence to the contrary. Genuine science is objective and open to correction as the evidence presents itself. Talking snakes, global floods and the existence of a supreme being who's concerned about what humans do with their genitals requires evidence to become scientifically credible. Science eliminates anything leading to erroneous conclusions. The belief in a Supreme Being or life after death can affect an individual's perceptions, thoughts and behaviour, so without scientific safeguards these beliefs have a high probability of distorting research. Such beliefs will also have a significant influence on how they treat other people, their children, and how they govern a country. In the words of the famous rocket scientist Carl Sagan, *"Extraordinary claims require extraordinary evidence."* You'll not find a genuine scientist making a claim without objective research, number crunching, and peer review. Scientists make predictions based on existing facts, testable against reality. We didn't land people on the moon through prayer and hope, but through exact mathematical calculations. Scientists noticed a gravitational effect in our solar system indicating an unknown planet. Clyde Tombaugh used these calculations to aim his telescope in the right direction and find Pluto. The gravitational effect of Pluto could only be caused by a large mass of rock, ice and gas. If the scientists found Pluto was made of strawberry blancmange, then they would update their understanding of puddings, but weren't necessary. Scientists have used similar principles to determine whether Dark Matter makes up a large proportion of the universe. Like Pluto, they can't see it, but know it's there by its effect. Scientists don't know what mass is making up dark matter, and because they don't have enough information to identify what it's, they refrain from a conclusion. It's rather like a child finding a cave. Some children will be curious and look inside the cave. Some children will be too afraid to enter the cave because they imagine a dragon is there. Scientists look at dark

Matter and don't know what it's and so continue to research they do not assume it's anything. For some spiritually inclined people, they may view dark matter as the heavenly world filled with God, the angels, and the spirits of the dead. The difference between filling a gap with fantasy or a hypothetical idea is, fantasy is a desired reality, and a hypothesis is a suggested explanation changeable with evidence.

Counselling and psychotherapy developed from the scientific branch of psychology. Originally designed to study the mind, it has expanded to include personal development and manipulation techniques for business sales. One of the first books I read as a child was 'Bring Out the Magic in Your Mind' by Al Koran. This book was the starting point for my interest in psychology, but it was also a confusing stumbling block because it included a presentation of magical powers from the 'subconscious.' To my immature mind, this book seemed clever and therefore true. He mixed the power of the subconscious with 'magnetism', 'belief' and visualisation which he said would attract to the 'Mind Magician' anything they desired. He even attempted to give a warning regarding the certainty of the 'psychological Magic of the mind'. A warning example of its power was a woman who wanted to be waited on hand and foot for the rest of her life and got her wish when she took a major stroke and became paralysed. It wasn't a stone's throw away from the more recent nonsense of 'The Secret.' Al Koran included a little science and mixed it with spirituality. He included the sayings of Jesus and Buddha, promised empowerment, and was inspiring (to me anyway). Counselling and psychotherapy can inspire, creating a euphoric over-reaction to new insights. Some have likened their experience to a spiritual awakening, but the practices and philosophies of counselling are not spiritual in the metaphysical sense. The benevolent Carl Rogers didn't develop counselling by revelation, as he meditated around lotus flowers. The research contributing to psychotherapy involved the abuse of animals and children. The 'Little Albert' experiment, Harry Harlow's research on 'rhesus monkeys', and Martin Seligman's research into 'Learned helplessness' have assisted us to understand psychological malfunctions, but are ethically stomach wrenching for the Empath. The idea a cherished and benevolent profession could have abuse as part of its history is incompatible with our experiences. Like the mother who refuses to accept her son is a thief after a video presentation of him stealing lady's underwear from a washing line, it's easy to blind ourselves when it's incompatible with our beliefs. A love of science is not what attracts student counsellors. Cognitive Behavioural Therapy is the most scientific of the therapies and is used in counselling to great effect. It encourages a client to think objectively about their psychological triggers and how this relates to physical response and behaviour. Transactional Analysis, constructivism and Gestalt encourage the client to see their experience as a process and view it objectively and Jungian perspectives are also excellent at objectifying the process of mind, but a warping of psychological meanings is, occasionally, apparent in some people's understanding. I have heard people discuss Jung's idea of the collective unconscious as a form of telepathic communication rather than a common set of instinctual A priori knowledge. Humanistic psychology contributed to Person Centred Counselling providing the concept of Self -actualisation. Self-actualisation has been confused with spiritual awakening and the accompanying euphoria, rather than the experience of objective self-hood and autonomy textbooks discuss. Psychologists are scientists and are trained to think objectively without the influence of emotional bias. Counsellors by virtue of their empathic training are challenged in this area, and while many develop a good objective self, for a short time during training most counsellors lose objectivity for a while as they deal with deep personal issues and regrettably a minority never break out of the transcendent chrysalis and achieve an objective perspective. The difficulty with an applied psychological science like psychotherapy is it involves emotional aspects and counselling students might lose their ability to reason as the emotional exploration disrupts logical thinking for a time. When working with clients and other students in counselling it's easy to spot the student who has difficulty in staying in the client's 'frame of reference' as their own personal issues are triggered. If religion becomes the driving philosophy for counselling practice, there's a risk the approach will lose scientific credibility. Even Jesus said "a little leaven ferments the whole lump." Some Counsellors classify counselling as Christian without scientific data to support the assumption. They see a correlation in their own mind between the two subjects and use this observation to support their existing bias. Religious people misleading students about the credentials of their own spiritual viewpoint in psychotherapy are corrupting the source of its success. This makes students and anyone who is interested in personal development vulnerable to manipulation if they're rightly disposed. Students who embark on the study of counselling are generally damaged. It's rare to find a counselling student who has entered study without seeing the benefits of therapy in their own life. In the same way religious people take advantage of the emotionally damaged, who've suffered bereavement and suck them into their church. Pseudo-science has applied the same principles into psychotherapy and counselling with a large sprinkling of religious belief to mislead the masses. Over the past few decades pseudo-scientific philosophers such as Deepak Chopra have distorted the scientific principles of quantum mechanics to give credibility to their own spiritual approach. The research into quantum physics is fascinating and opens the door for much speculation regarding the mysterious effect of quantum duality; and although there are ideas put forward to explain these phenomena, all scientists agree, until we have more data, we need to accept we do not understand these strange effects. Spiritual pseudo-scientists latch onto the unknown elements of quantum theory and fill the gaps with 'the power of love,' 'Reiki' quantum healing, ghosts' and proof of the existence of spirits and gods. From the point of view of the average lost soul who longs for meaning, this sounds exciting, but to the level headed empiricist, it's absolutely 'baseless bonkers.' I don't have a problem with people believing in god or spiritual things as long as they don't distort effective scientifically created therapies with their need for succor and teach it as fact. Unfortunately, because the mind is a pattern matching machine, it's impossible for the spiritually minded person not to see their God manifest in anything appearing loving or virtuous.

Now, before I carry on talking about counselling and erroneous Christian ideas, I think it's important to clarify, I can't walk into a British town or village without seeing a Christian church. All British holidays are based on Christianity and schools are soaked in Christian tradition and not a law gets passed in the UK without the House of Lords, which has a high proportion of clergy having a disproportionate say in its passing. So if it seems like I'm picking Christianity in this book, it's because, in my country, Christianity is equally in your face as your own face. People are likely to see their god in anything they attribute as a godlike characteristic. Humility is a virtue in a lot of cultures, including Buddhism and any other religion condemning arrogance. It doesn't mean it was invented by a particular religion. A theist can't say, 'Hey, that's a Christian quality." What could be viewed as love is wonderfully described in intelligent terms by Carl Rogers, the founder of modern Counselling. He describes 'unconditional positive regard' to be like the love a mother has for her child, but it's exasperating to find the Christian mind correlating this to the love of Christ who accepts anyone who repents, even though repentance has conditions attached. It's enough to make you weep when faced with a committed Christian who always sees the science through the goggles of God. The goggles of god 'cloud everything'. For many, God is an absolute, and exists without question. This kind of belief must permeate throughout an individual's perception of reality. They see God in all existence. In fact, it's not called existence in the theist eyes; rather, it's called creation. Some beliefs naturally follow a belief in a God. When people find meaning in 'creation,' then they also find meaning in their own lives. They may even find God offers them immortality and power to do magic through prayer. All the benefits coming with a belief in God require 'faith,' the antithesis of science. Some people suggest scientists have faith in the process of the scientific process. It can be an exasperating exercise to explain the scientific process involving testing a hypothesis and trying to disprove it. It involves an unbiased approach to examining verifiable data and repeating the process so different researchers can verify it. Human knowledge is acquired through empirical experience or 'through the senses.' So faith in this sense is the only thing scientists could be accused of having, but technically they don't have faith in their own senses, they use objective verification of their findings, to make sure they weren't hallucinating or perhaps lying their pants off. The difference between spiritual training and scientific empiricism is that a scientific approach requires the repetition of an experiment by different people in order to confirm a truth, and if a finding is repeatedly found to be false, then the belief is changed. Generally , spirituality, religion and a belief in God means an individual will absolutely reject any evidence to the contrary and recognise only supporting evidence. The great philosopher Obiwan said, *"Only a Sith thinks in absolutes."* When young Luke Skywalker asked Master Yoda "is the dark side stronger?" he simply answered, *"No, but it's easily the more seductive."* Even though Master Yoda was a rubber Muppet, his words could have been applied to any belief system promising a sense of control, structure and hope in the face of contrary evidence. Religion is seductive because it provides a sense of safety and if we feel safe, our mind can focus on happier things. Humans crave comfort and embrace denial like a five-year-old who finds it difficult to accept he moved during the game 'musical statues.'

Thinking in absolutes is dangerous because it means our mind is not open to evidence based on change. Humans have a tendency to ignore anything disturbing the status quo. Warn a village about an erupting volcano and there'll be people who'll stay in their house and watch the TV in the belief it will be alright. In America there's a large proportion of people who are ignoring the evidence regarding climate change by focusing on erroneous evidence such as 'a chilly day disproves theories of global warming.' The people who spread this kind of misinformation have their own agenda, to please the energy companies or the electorate who long for comfort. The belief is absolute and not open to change. A mother was surprised to find her thirteen-year-old son had acquired an expensive stunt scooter one day. She asked him where he gained it and was happy to hear he found it discarded in a park. When the police knocked at her door to arrest her son and return the Scooter back to its rightful owner, she refused to believe her son had stolen it. People always have an incentive for believing lies, especially when it fulfills some need for comfort. Lies and untruths are seductive because they offer something difficult to attain elsewhere and something is security and comfort. People are suckers for it. When you watch a general election unfold, it's easy to predict who the winner will be. The charismatic leader can gain support by looking pretty. In fact, as I write I can't think of an election where the charismatic candidate has been defeated by a bland personality. This is because people are generally shallow and easily led by superficial judgements and preference. Oh, and they're also led by flattery. People feel magnificent when they are flattered. They'll come back for more. Feed the flatterer with whatever they want (at varying degrees) to gain more flattery. The gentleman who seduces a woman tells her she is beautiful. It feels good, and the woman may even feel like she is in love and give him his wild oats (if that's the right term). Religious proselytizers are no different, they tell those weighed down with low self-esteem that Jesus loves them 'so much' he allowed himself to be tortured and killed as a human sacrifice to pay for their sinful state. How charitable of him. People will believe any old rubbish if it fits with their needs. Maslow produced the hierarchy of needs to describe what motivates people, and it's this that can probably explain why people so easily lead down the garden path of deceit (whether self-deceit or the deliberate deceit of another). Some people suggest, 'the truth hurts,' but it's probably more accurate to say 'truth helps us grow' (although it doesn't roll off the tongue with the same poetic grace.) The truth helps us grow because it's when faced with reality, we can deal with it pragmatically. Death is a bugger. In my childhood I woke up in the night, scared by the realisation of my own inevitable death. My mother explained I would go to heaven where everything is super. A lovely belief to get me to sleep. The well-adjusted people I have known are atheists. I am sure the reason for their maturity is they learned to live with life's uncertainties without the comfort of fables, however a belief in a higher power helps overcome addictions to alcohol and other substances. The '12 steps' Alcoholics Anonymous program puts the belief in a higher power into therapeutic use. If I believe splashing water from the River Tyne on my face will cure a tense headache, then my belief is validated when the pain subsides. I don't mean to devalue the work of the AA, but any placebo is effective when the power of belief is active. Hypnosis is a great inducer of the placebo effect. We put faith in hypnotherapists and their techniques and suddenly we're cured of social anxiety, smoking or some other malady reducing our quality of life. A higher power is someone who claims to have a higher power, and this could include anyone we put faith in. It need not be a God, it can be a doctor, counsellor, acupuncturist, hypnotherapist, policeman, teacher, politician or manager. We can see all these people as a higher power, and their opinions and abilities are most times perceived to be greater than the average person. It's not unusual to be involved in a discussion with someone who wants to make a point with little evidence and will resort to presenting credibility to their belief by stating 'the local doctor uses the technique of sticking lemons up your nose to cure eczema and it appears to have worked for Mrs Jones, who is a respected member of the Woman's Guild.' A respected position and great rhetoric can charm the birds from the trees. Religion has used the placebo effect and shallow psychological tricks to seduce the masses since the beginning of humanity. It's terrifying to see the tool of charisma that can convince people to become suicide bombers or vote fascists into power and sign up for direct debit payments for cable television. I'm not saying everyone has been seduced by a charismatic leader, but it's likely one of your ancestors was converted and you inherited their religion. Every family that holds their religion close to their hearts has an ancestor who was gullible or who was intelligent but tortured until they converted. Sorry if I offend, but to my shame, I have licence to make such a statement because I have stood amongst the ranks of the most gullible people on the planet. It's true, counsellors normally enter their training as sensitive neurotics looking for answers, and I was no different.

MY NEUROTIC JOURNEY TO CREDULITY.

So why am I so bothered? Atheists are accused of being angry at God, hating God, but that'd be daft. I discovered Santa Claus doesn't exist at nine years old and I'm not angry at him any more than I'm angry at the 'tooth fairy' (although she did short change me for one of my front teeth). I don't believe God exists, and I am angry at myself (perhaps) for wasting years of my life devoted to fiction, but I can't be angry at him (God), any more than I can be angry at Odin, Zeus or Scooby Doo. I could be angry at the churches and the religious/spiritual leaders, but the leaders are as blind as the followers, so it's sensible to view them all as victims. As the great atheist, Jesus said, "if the blind follows the blind, they'll both fall in the pit." People who can see truth or at least recognise gaps in evidence are usually the ones who appreciate objectivity, recognise bias in perception and respect the scientific process. If there's anything to be angry at, it's probably the tendency of some humans who'll feed each other 'pain killing poison of lies' rather than embark on an adventure into the unknown. We cannot blame humans for their attraction to comforting lies. The hope it brings engenders hope and relief from suffering, but it also makes us its slaves. You can't give your life to religion without sacrificing your moral compass. Religion makes its followers into slaves; it even decides what you can think and when you should feel ashamed. Jesus said, *"The truth shall make you free,"* but Jesus rejected organized religion and the burdens it places on its people. Buddha is attributed as saying "Believe nothing, No matter where you read it, or who has said it, not even if I have said it, unless it agrees with your own reason and your own common sense." The absolute truth is not a reasonable goal. There'll always be gaps in knowledge filled with bollocks, and there's more speculation and misplaced trust in our minds' library of knowledge than anything else. One of the greatest lures of religion is, it offers the promises of absolute truth and makes ignorance a virtue.

I became a counsellor after a long spell of faith-based neurosis. I will not deny it, I was looking for meaning to life in my early years and eventually gave up and joined the first fundamentalist Christian sect rearing its head and offering a reasonably sounding argument. The search for meaning in life and the universe was probably my first mistake as it ignored the possibility there's no objective meaning at all. In my enthusiasm to find a 'black cat in a dark room that isn't there', I began my search. I didn't consider nor did it occur to me that something could exist without meaning, but like a potential buyer of a Jackson Pollock painting in a car boot fair, I was determined to find meaning in the mess of reality. I had never considered if there was meaning to the universe that it might not be findable on the minutely finite confines of the insignificantly sized Earth. I decided accepting unverifiable nonsense was better than nothing. Counselling didn't introduce me to an atheist/ scientific mind. It took roughly two years after training for me to discover the problem with my mind is over thinking and the inability to recognise and dismiss erroneous beliefs. My atheist conclusion was probably and ironically down to my studies in Buddhism.

As a baby, I was baptized a Catholic at St Paul's in Cramlington. My Father's Family were all Anglican, but because my mother's family were all religious, I was baptised Catholic and attended Sunday mass until I received my first Holy Communion at the age of eight. My mother felt she had fulfilled her obligation to raise me as a Catholic and immediately got a cleaning job in a factory, and to my relief I was no longer required to attend church every Sunday morning and could watch Thunderbirds on TV instead. My Father was a Freemason in those days. I'm not sure what significance this has, as the only sign he was a member of anything remotely odd was when I found him trying on an

Apron with jewels on it. It was the Mason Apron with strange occult imagery with special meaning to the affiliated, however; I was 8 years old and just assumed he was a cross dresser. The TV provided a regular dose of fantasy and supernatural shows which combined with strange hallucinations during measles, mumps and tonsillitis, episodes of multiple incredible hulks filling my bedroom and witches appearing at my window on broomsticks. Witches and multiple Hulks in my bedroom were a production of a mind generating hallucinations because of the serious need of some paracetamol; however I decided it must have some spiritual aspect to it, in the same way someone who takes magic mushrooms considers that believing you can fly might have meaning. Around the same time I woke up in the middle of the night and saw a Turkish gentleman wearing a turban or some kind of similar looking big hat standing at my bedroom door holding a blood covered knife. I thought it was a ghost, but on reflection as an adult I reckon it was probably a dream. It wasn't an intruder, as our Betamax video recorder was still there in the morning. My next apparition happened after I conducted an Ouija board with one of my friends at 10 years old. Neil Stewart was about 9 years old and because I was 10, and he wanted to be my friend, he believed I was more intelligent than I was and he believed anything I said. We had no instructions on how to conduct such an activity and resorted to placing a glass upside down on a mirror. We both agreed that 'Ouija' must be a spirit and if we repeated the word 'Ouija' enough times the spirit would be summoned and kindly move the glass. You understand, in those days there was no internet to tell you how to do it properly and the best advice we could find was usually guesswork or an episode of Hammer House of Horror. In fact if you wanted to acquire any kind of knowledge in those days you would need to visit publicly funded libraries which never supplied a good Occult section. Nowadays kids are spoilt with the amount of knowledge they've available to them. Just type into Google "how do you conduct an Ouija?" and you not only get instructions, but you can also print the bloody Ouija board out. I would've given my right arm for that. As I slept I was woken in the early hours by a bright light shining through my window and my name repeatedly whispered loudly. The fear gripped me as I froze and begged the voice to call my Friend's name instead. The voice ignored my pleas and unmercifully continued repeating my name, "Alexander, Alexander, Alexander." I go by the name Alex now because there are far fewer syllables in the name, and because of this event I feel it sounds less sinister. I fell asleep without seeking the protection of my parents, suggesting I was dreaming, but that's not as exciting. Neil and I gave a title to our research into these apparitions; it became 'The Case of the Witch.' We weren't too sure how to begin the investigation or even why we'd called it 'The case of the Witch', but we both agreed following old ladies around our local shopping centre would be a good start at identifying a witch and discovering the answer to our experiences. After several weeks of surveillance, we discovered an old lady who'd struggle to do her shopping in the Presto supermarket. We also noticed she would buy bread and milk and sometimes laxatives. We attributed her purchases as evidence of witchcraft. After shopping, she would visit the shop café and enjoy a coffee and scone in the company of two gentlemen in their 70s. But who were these mysterious male companions? A man would sit in the Presto's café staring out of the window with what we interpreted as intent, but intent on doing what? We had a bias to perceive the uncanny, and the uncanny we would perceive, do or die. We decided the man should be called 'The Watcher,' for his suspicious nature of, well, watching. The Witch's other friend was also around 70ish and had a white beard. He looked like a Fisherman and gave him the name 'The Fisherman's Friend'. And so we'd discovered the coven. Nothing else interesting happened for a while, and so my friend tried to communicate with the witch. He nervously walked over to her in the bread isle of Presto and with a quivering voice asked a skilled question. "Excuse me, could you tell me where I can find bread?" I looked through the window of the shop at my friend bravely putting his life in danger to gain more information that could lead to esoteric knowledge. He stepped outside the shop and looked at me with fear in his eyes. "Her breath smelled of mint," he exclaimed as he hyperventilated. The mint in her breath could only mean she was mixing herbs as part of a potion. The thought she was possibly sucking a Polo mint didn't fit with what we wanted to find, so we ignored it. There was no doubt we now had proof. She was a Witch and The Watcher and Fisherman's Friend were warlocks. This discovery didn't bring me closer to understanding the meaning of life and the universe. I still assumed there was meaning, we were determined to understand it. We believed for a short time these innocent people had supernatural powers, which as children was of no consequence, but had we been Adults in a medieval world they would probably have been burned at the stake with the evidence we presented. That's the genuine power and influence of religion. It can take an adult and make them behave like infantile children, who've difficulty differentiating between fantasy and reality. When I was about 10 years old, my friend Anthony presented me with his mother's packet of Tarot Cards. I think they were French by design. He told me they could predict the future and read people's minds. They fascinated me. He also had a thin piece of red clear plastic in the shape of a fish which rests on the palm of your hand. This fish would curl and bend in distinct shapes as it reacted to the heat of your hand or perhaps static electricity in the plastic (I'm not sure which). But anyway, I saw what I perceived to be a miracle and wanted a pack of Tarot Cards for myself to guide me through life and reveal to me the meaning of life, the universe and everything. I mentioned Anthony's Tarot cards to my friend Stu Wharrier. Stu Wharrier looked a little like Harry Potter. He had the same hair and glasses. Speaking with him was like speaking with a child professor. He was an Atheist and entertained by beliefs in the supernatural, but always suspended judgement regarding its reality. He said he had some fortune cards and some books on the occult he could supply me with for my investigations. Fortune cards were Lenormand cards, usually found in trinket shops in coastal villages. They had a picture and poem on each card which gave clues to their meaning when placed next to each other they can create a story presented as a prediction. Stu was always scientific in his perspective, and although he found occult matters interesting, he was never gullible enough to be fooled. Stu was a little more relaxed regarding what he didn't know and always used to refer back to the scientific method we'd learned in school. He realised if you truly trust the scientific method you can perform great miracles, which he demonstrated by setting another scientifically minded friend on fire. Both of them had discussed the chemical qualities of Peter's coat. They were convinced it was fire retardant and would withstand the heat of burning lighter fluid. Peter was so convinced this was the case, he volunteered to wear the coat as it was burning. Stu took the lighter fluid and the matches and passed it to a lad called Paul. I knew Paul for his tendency to entertain us by taking risks. Paul covered Peter in lighter fluid and lit a match, throwing it in Peter's direction. Peter then became a bright light of flame. It was funny at first until we realised Paul had applied more lighter fluid than Stu and Peter had entered in their computations. Eventually, the flames began bellowing out black smoke. Stu hypothesized the fire retardant material was no longer viable and immediately kicked Peter to the ground, and we gathered around him, beating him with our coats until the flames abated. Peter emerged from his coat unscathed and wearing the smile of a bungee jumper who thought they would die, and exclaimed, "Well, it was a calculated risk." Apart from being risked with their science, they were the most gifted scholars you could meet. Peter achieved a PhD in something, I can't remember what. My studies in the Occult and divination became frustratingly deep. I say frustratingly, because they yielded no wisdom and the Tarot cards offered little in the way of insight, although Stu's advice on using the symbolism in the cards prepared me to become an effective Cold Reader which was a skill I used at charity fairs. My family organised these Charity fairs, and it surprised me to find how easy it was to be viewed as accurate. Most people who visit a fortune-teller are likely to respond positively to generalised guesses. The Theists will believe the vague predictions found in their Bible and find credibility by taking the generalised descriptions and specifically attribute them to current events in history. I need to emphasise, I wasn't aware at the time I was using Cold Reading techniques. I knew there was a certain amount of guesswork involved, but suspected my success could be attributed to a certain amount of spiritual power. So I continued blindly looking for the source of this power, which I assumed to be a God. Eventually the Gideon's visited our school. The Gideon's is the organisation that leaves Bibles in hotel rooms. They left free copies of the New Testament for all the pupils, which I grabbed and read. It was interesting, Jesus appeared to come up with some inspiring sayings, and it featured the Book of Revelation in many of the Tarot Cards I had used. I was gullible and another close friend of mine was a member of an American influenced Church. After talking with him for a few hours about the Bible, I was determined to follow Jesus and together we burned my Tarot cards in his back garden. A few days later the euphoria died down, and I felt lost. I spoke to Stu about my introduction to Jesus and the burning of the Cards. He looked at me shocked, "You get too excited. You have been questioning the meaning of life for years, and you throw 'who you are' away without examining what you've accepted." The search for meaning had become a hunger for meaning at any cost. This lesson wasn't learned well. After absorbing myself in Hare Krishna books, The Koran and The Upanishads for several years, I eventually committed to joining an authoritarian Christian Group whose power lay in their ability to make nonsense sound sensible to 'the rightly disposed'. The rightly disposed person was me. Inevitably, I would join a religion like the Jehovah's witnesses. My inability to recognise my own fraudulent ability to read people's cards as nothing more than cold reading would mean I could easily accept the blind guides as spiritual gurus and willingly allow them to seduce me into their church with the promise of absolute truth. My Journey into the Jehovah's Witness Religion started after I was married. I was 21 and my dad showed an interest in the Religion after his wife joined some years before. I heard the JW rhetoric from my dad and eventually accepted the invitation to study with some members of the congregation and quickly started attending their meetings. Their pseudo-scientific arguments impressed me against evolution and their explanations regarding the meaning of life. I was satisfied I had found the truth. Studies with JW's were a constant bombardment of information. The Bible was recited and sang about. I studied their literature to prepare for 3 meetings a week when a question and answer session would take place. There was also additional training and preparation for preaching work. They trained me to prepare and deliver talks on The Bible and eventually saw the universe through God Goggles. I enjoyed the sport of arguing with educated people regarding their belief in science and evolution, and would constantly research arguments supporting my beliefs, and would destroy the beliefs of others. I did this in the hope I could validate my faith through converting someone who is a respected and intelligent member of the community. I was unsuccessful, but alienated people who were nice by tactfully and sometimes abruptly telling them the Bible condemned them to death unless they joined my church. The attitude 'this is a lifesaving work' and anyone outside the faith will be executed by God on the fiery day of Armageddon meant being a little rude was acceptable when preaching and to save the ones we love when they refuse to follow the rules there was a provision of excommunication. Known as shunning, this involves ignoring children and adults as if they're dead, an effective way to return people to the fold. The way love was expressed disillusioned me. To make sure children are protected from God's wrath, the JW church would use some odd methods. If a child left the JW's, then they were placing themselves outside God's protection and opening themselves up to Satan's world. To persuade them to return to the safety of the JW church, they were disfellowshipped (excommunicated). Excommunication is an effective way to control a child's mind. They're taught that anyone outside the church is 'part of Satan's world' so they only form close attachments with those in the fold. The result of being disfellowshipped is exile. The sinner is dangerous and orders are given to shun the sinner. The parents and siblings of the sinner were to reduce contact with them to the bare minimum, hoping 'they would come to their senses." To anyone viewing this from the outside, it would appear to be bullying, but any form of abuse in the spirit of love was viewed by the JW's as beneficial. Like most forms of emotional abuse, disfellowshipping relies on the child's (and the adults') fear of abandonment for it to be successful in forcing people to return to the fold. People who had joined the JW's could leave and be undamaged by their experience, but children who had formed no attachments outside the JW's are vulnerable to the effects of this abuse because they've learned from an early age to view the outside world as sexually promiscuous, drug taking psychopaths. After one 15-year-old girl was disfellowshipped, it became apparent she was finding affection from any source available to her. She had been conditioned from infancy; the world is full of criminals, drug addicts and sexual deviants. These were the people she found acceptance with and helped her deal with emotional pain. After mothering 5 children, she eventually lost them all as social services swooped in to protect them from the extraordinary world they were living in. Other girls (always the girls who fared badly after excommunication) experienced a similar fate unless they were lucky. I worked hard in the church by studying and preaching. Eventually I gained a promotion in the church to Ministerial Servant, but instead of becoming proud of my position I became more disillusioned as time went on. The Elders and Ministerial Servants found power and influence in the fold of an artificial society of predisposed sheep. The more dogmatic and unquestioning you were, the more successful you could become. As they climbed the ranks in a church offering little reward except hope, men could also work toward possessing power over the vulnerable. Although some of these men had good intentions, they were forced to exercise the will of their Governing Body or lose their position. The promise of prominence seduced me, but my criticism of some of JW's methods, such as baptizing older children with the prospect of abandoning them if they deviated from the path, was a major concern to me. To be part of a group willing to coerce families to reduce contact with their children was too much for me to live up to. Owing to my inability to control my mouth, I expressed my indignation to the local elders and quickly lost some important responsibilities, and my cynical reason for remaining in the JW church disappeared. I worry that if they had kept feeding my ego, my departure from the church may never have happened. Would I have kept my conscience quiet in favour of reward? That's a significant question I will never know the answer to. Psychopathology is a common characteristic of the successful executive. Empathy or a conscience isn't an effective characteristic if you want success. If you're guided by natural empathy, it's unlikely you'll toe the party line unless you can ignore those naturally ethical promptings. If statistics are right then like corporate business, you may find the leadership of religion has a high chance of being led by narcissists. The Catholic Church has a long history of pope sanctioned torture and genocide. Even when they could slow down the spread of HIV and Aids, they maintained their authority instead. People are always reluctant to criticise authority to protect their own position. It's just a natural trait. The greatest difficulty is if your hierarchy of authority begins with an unchangeable book like the Bible or the Koran. You can leave feedback for a book on Amazon and tell everyone your opinion of the writing. Trust me. It can be a painful experience, but the Bible and the Koran are two books that can cause the critic's death. There are many examples of philosophers, heretics and scientists who've offered their own appraisal for the Bible which has resulted in their death. Criticizing the Bible is equal to criticizing God and his God appointed henchmen will exercise his righteous wrath with extreme prejudice to maintain their own position. This explains why we're not as different from apes. The leader ape is the most physically aggressive and powerful. They got into their position by fighting other males for the position and won. The other males willingly surrender to his authority out of fear rather than their respect for the alpha male's expression of empathy and compassion. Humans are the same and holding the book in the air and claiming actions are based in the Bible or Koran gives the illusion of righteousness. To the religious leader it acts as a contract between the parishioner and God, and they're the authority who decides how the scriptures are interpreted. And that was my disillusionment with the JW church. It wasn't all bad though. They gave me the opportunity to learn to prepare talks and deliver them. They also gave me the opportunity to conduct Bible study groups. The result was I grew in confidence and considered taking my learning further in college. The subjects I chose in college were psychology and counselling. Like most counselling students, I began reading inspiring literature with therapeutic philosophies. There was a lot of rubbish on the bookshelves, but one subject appeared to be intelligent and in its original form closely related to subjects I had studied in psychotherapy. The subject I began reading was Buddhism.

I was in the Scottish Border town of Hawick and found one of Thich Nhat Hanh's books being sold as surplus stock from a library. I realised Buddhism was more of a philosophy than a religion. Caroline Brazier's book 'Buddhist psychology' expanded on this by discussing the Skandhas or aggregates coalesce our being and perception. The ideas were familiar to me and reminiscent of Gestalt therapy and cognitive psychology. Humans are made of multiple parts, even the parts of our parts appear to have separate parts. We have the senses to see, hear and smell. We have thoughts and perceptions and memories working together, but when one is missing the human will still function. MRI scans on the brains of humans have detected that even our mind behaves as separate parts, and personality is not a constant. We can even prove the production of hormones appears to contribute to our behaviour and thinking, and to change any aspect of the human can change the whole dynamic interaction of these parts. This brought about a concept of the nonself. If I am a collection of many parts, then I have no essence or central self. Consciousness appears to create the illusion of self and consequently protects the whole organism from harm. This brief explanation of a complicated subject appeared to make the search for immortality in a spirit world futile. Consciousness is nothing more than an effect of processing information. Bit nihilistic, but that's reality. If anyone says we're more than this, I would like to hear the argument. 'I feel real,' is a by-product of consciousness and not a rational argument. Ironically, the religion of Buddhism was leading me to Atheism. The idea I don't exist or have a central essence makes it a lot easier to no longer possess a belief in God. Accepting you might not exist is upsetting for some, but Buddhism recommends meditation. In meditation you can quieten the mind. Now, the human mind likes to think, but until I practised meditation, I didn't realise how annoying the mind is. It's constantly talking like an old woman who never gets visitors. It talks about any old crap it can think of. During meditation, the realisation hits you, 'I am not my mind, because I am observing my mind as it chatters away independently of my will." I found through independent practice of Mindfulness meditation the mind's chatter can be silenced, but difficult to sustain without practice. Buddhist teachers recommend focusing the mind on the sensations of breathing. The mind naturally wanders and starts processing problems, making plans, worrying and losing focus. Then you return your mind to the breath. I would meditate with a notepad and record any thought distracting me. It was amazing to read the list at the end of the session. They were presented with a list of decreasingly unimportant demands on my thinking time. Absolutely pointless anxiety producing thoughts. For example, as I meditated, the thought popped into my head, 'I've run out of milk.' sure enough the fridge needed to be replenished with milk, but meditation made me aware of the physical sensation of anxiety accompanying the thought. The practice made the relationship between mind and body clearer to me more than any study of textbooks could accomplish. Objectively observing my thoughts was possibly the strangest thing I have experienced, because it now appears a new and transcendent consciousness has come into existence for the duration of the session. After the session, the experience stopped. The observant self had no thoughts itself; rather, it just allowed everything else to exist without judgement or the desire to change it. The search for meaning then became ridiculous to me. There was no reason to search for meaning because I don't exist. Without thought, desire, sorrow or pain. These things were just temporary experiences. The experience was one of peace. The minimal process of focusing on the breath was the most inspiring educator I have known. The thing I will regret about the silence of death is I cannot process its peace. But perhaps processing peace is meaningless. The desire for peace is like the desire for death. As we meditate all we are is silenced. Buddhists spend their last moments in mindfulness, experiencing their death in its reality as the observer, as the mind is silenced in its peaceful nirvana state for eternity. However, I keep returning to neurosis, 'oh well keep practising,' I keep telling myself, and I realise I don't have a self. Buddhist studies lead me to Atheism. Buddhism has no God and asks practitioners to be mindful of their own empirical existence and not the perceptions we hold. Science encourages us to approach reality similarly. To test ideas in different conditions with different people with differing biases. Science establishes what's probably true and changes with the evidence. I liked that. As I researched Atheism, I discovered most scientists are Atheists. This is something I should have been able to work out long before I was 31 years old. I couldn't differentiate real science from fraud. Science is a way of thinking. It means you'll recognise how bias colours your perception. It also means you'll need to consider the evidence of other people's experiences and be prepared to settle for not knowing the answer to some questions. Science requires objectivity and mindfulness. It's not the role of science to be comforting or peaceful, and if that was its purpose then it wouldn't be creating laser guns and photon torpedoes. Its purpose is to seek truth in the most reliable way possible. When I began counselling professionally it became obvious that many people suffer because they can't think objectively. Any strategy for encouraging the client to observe themselves objectively was insightful. Transactional Analysis, gestalt and Cognitive therapy were excellent in assisting clients to strengthen objectivity and regain a sense of control. In fact, anything assisting the client to recognise and work with different aspects of self is useful in therapy. Counselling is not there to provide comfort, it's there to help an individual live as effectively as possible within their reality. In the words of Jacob Marley when hearing Scrooge's plea for comfort, "I have none to give." Jacob Marley was visiting his old friend to give him the chance to develop compassion and love of life. Scrooge had become bitter and too focused on money and work. He resented the poor and rejected friendship and family. He changed after his visitations by the Ghosts. Even though he had no hope of an afterlife, his death would involve fewer regrets for a wasted life. Perhaps that's the true meaning of life. Don't waste it, live it in its entirety and value the people in it. Leave a legacy making the world grow in your absence. There's nothing else.

How do we know what's true?

David Hume was a Scottish philosopher who realised, rather like the Buddha, we obtain all knowledge through the senses. If an individual is without senses, they can't know if they're hungry or a hug can be comforting. Without senses, there's nothing. Hume's philosophy was empiricism, and he argued nothing is known without the senses and because the senses are open to false perceptions, bias reasoning, inaccurate memories and hallucination, even this is not ideal. Empiricism and awareness of its limits form the basis for scientific investigation. Hume recognised there was no empirical evidence for the existence of God but stopped short of declaring his atheism because such a view was against Scottish law and would result in execution. The German philosopher Immanuel Kant discussed A Priori knowledge, which is pre-programmed into the brain at birth. This knowledge is the basis for understanding the knowledge entering the senses after we are born. A Priori knowledge is anything innate. A newly born child has A Priori programming makes it behave in a specific way when encountering specific stimuli. It will cry on hearing a loud noise, it will cry and make sucking gestures when hungry, it will react to pain or discomfort with vocalizations and physical movements, especially when experiencing colic. Jung believed we have archetypes pre-programed into our minds. They are innate parts of the mind, predisposed to acquiring specific information. Not necessarily knowledge, but they're like an empty folder on a computer allocated to store specific information. One folder could be called Mother and another folder could be called danger, yet another folder could be called danger. The 'mother folder' is filled with memories, pictures and phrases maternal figures in life express. Perhaps there's a reference or shortcut in the folder that opens the safe folder and the child can associate the maternal figure with safety or perhaps danger, depending on their experience. We have innate templates guiding us to acquire knowledge, and this knowledge can colour perceptions. If a child experiences an abusive maternal figure, it's possible this knowledge will inform future relationships with people who've similar characteristics and may result in strong emotional reactions. Sigmund Freud called such correlations 'Transference' and made it a central tenet of his therapy. Newly gained information is influenced by previous learning. Our perceptions and learning are also influenced by our needs. The need for food, water, sex, money, respect, power, domination are all examples of needs and desires affecting how and what's perceived. Maslow put forward the hierarchy of needs which he believed would influence behaviour. A person may be motivated to eat and find food if they're starving, they'll also be predisposed to recognise food that wasn't in the person's awareness before. For the starving individual, a discarded sandwich in a bin or dog food will be perceived as a menu option and exist in the foreground of the mind, whereas for the rest of us, this would not be thinkable. A child who attends a new school may well be more than ready to perceive a potential friend, foe or protective parental figure. Whatever is in the foreground of our minds such as unfulfilled needs is the filter of Perception and the basis of learning. Carl Rogers observed that his clients appeared to adapt their values and beliefs in order to be accepted and loved by a family, spouse or peer group. These beliefs have varying degrees of influence on an individual's thinking and behaviour and permeate throughout the individual's perception of reality. This type of belief would be learned by listening to the teaching of other humans in the desired social group. In order to be accepted and avoid rejection, the individual will adapt their values and beliefs to feel secure.

This is not surprising. If a catholic child in Northern Ireland decides he would now like to become an Anglican, there's a possibility his family will be aggressive in their opposition to prevent their son's conversion. There are some with beliefs that are positive and helpful, and people generally access counselling because they've been introjected (or adopted without examination), beliefs and values that result in maladaptive behaviour and distressing emotions. The conscience is supplemented by beliefs and values. Religious communities are awash with rules and beliefs which demand members not only conform to a set of behaviours but should also alter their thinking to match. Even the most liberal of religions require a certain amount of compliance from their members, except for the Anglican Church who are just grateful if people turn up once in a while. Religion offers the love of God in exchange for behavioural and psychological compliance. Parents and our social group are hard enough to please, but a God could scribble you out of the scroll of life for allowing sexual thoughts to exist and the sincere believer is reminded by their bible trained conscience. Religion controls, behaviour, thinking and emotions.

At the risk of repeating myself: Counselling is a profession which is based on science. In fact, the science of psychology has strict ethical principles that have been developed by humans who are guided by natural empathy and intelligent reasoning. Some faith-based counsellors base their theory on the conditional love of a holy book teaching judgement, hatred and the promise of death to those who reject its teaching. Yes, it's true some spiritual counselling incorporates an amount of scientifically based theory, but then they contaminate it with their own bias interpretations, in effect perverting its use and de-emphasising the unpalatable parts of their faith's teaching. Effective counselling requires the practitioner to have certain qualities difficult to develop without intensive training and therapy or an upbringing involving unconditional love. Religion and faith do not provide such an upbringing, in fact, religion has churned out a high density of 'fucked up people' into the arms of genuine therapists who are all too familiar with the dangers of dogma and the anxieties induced by spiritual communities using threats of abandonment to control their minds. The core qualities of a counsellor should always include a developed ability to experience empathy and express this to the client without adding the "how I would feel in your position" element to the situation. Unfortunately there are counsellors who believe their own personal experience will enhance their empathy and as a result begin to confuse the client's experience with their own. Such symptoms are caused by failing to work through personal issues thoroughly enough before helping others. Even if we think our own experiences have medicinal qualities the fact is, it can contaminate the therapeutic process. Another core value of counselling is the counsellor's state of congruence. This state involves being honest to oneself and to the client. It means being integrated and authentic, without a mask to hide our real thoughts and intentions. This might be difficult if we believe the way to mental health is to guide someone to Jesus. Another quality the counsellor will have is unconditional acceptance. This sounds easy until we encounter a client who does not share our values and beliefs. If we're offended by a client's beliefs it's difficult to accept them as they are. And if we do not accept a client unconditionally with 'warts n all' then how can we ever hope to see the world from their frame of reference. How can someone with faith in Christianity offer counselling to a Muslim, a homosexual or an Atheist, if they truly believe these people deserve to die in Armageddon? People of faith cannot apply their faith in a scientifically based profession without losing credibility. The counsellor's use of self is emphasised in all counselling courses, which means they use their training empathy and communication skills to encourage exploration and insight. Use of self does not mean introducing faith or personal experience, as a good counsellor will keep their own 'ego' with all the values and beliefs accompanying such a concept outside the therapy room. The wise counsellor will recognise the 'ego' and learn to place it in a hypothetical context. Many never reach that level of professionalism and become a 'shut-eye' in the face of their own personal biases. A counsellor will inhibit the client's progress if they enter the room with their own agenda for joining the profession. Some will join the profession intending to wear an ego of benevolence, who want to become a guru or emulate their religious prophets such as Jesus, the Dalai Lama or Russell Brand. Although this might sound unkind, the power of ego comes with its own set of biases and potential problems. If we arrive as a counsellor intending to feed an ego or to act as a 'wounded healer' who hasn't healed himself, then the focus will not be on the client, everything will be seen through the eyes of your own 'shit'. Some people may take offence at the word 'shit' being used in a book describing the therapeutic approach, but the word 'issues' doesn't describe the negative effect of the therapist's own agenda intruding on the client's therapeutic hour. Counsellors must learn to become a blank slate and develop an understanding of what it means to present a nonself. To be an objective individual who reflects the facts for the client to evaluate, rather than a wise old guru who thinks they've esoteric knowledge to share. What has this all got to do with atheism?, atheism is seen by many as a belief system with Richard Dawkins as its leader, making its purpose to shut down faith schools and remove religion from politics. This view on Atheism is because it contains the suffix 'ism' and is reminiscent of belief systems and valuing systems such as Catholicism, Buddhism, Communism and Hinduism and perhaps for some, Thatcherism. Atheism is different; it contains no beliefs or values, although atheists may adopt a philosophy or develop their own personal ethics based on natural empathy and altruism. Atheism is the absence of a belief in God, and that's it. Oddly enough, this does not mean you hold a belief God is non-existent, although you might. It rather means you don't have God as a belief (think about it). For example, Tom tells you, Lady Gaga is a man. You might like Tom and have no reason to doubt him, but because Tom provides little evidence for his belief, you choose not to accept this information as fact. This doesn't mean you have dismissed the story as a fallacy, but it means you can suspend judgement. Likewise, atheists do not accept a belief in God as there's no genuine evidence to believe it. Most atheists admit that if they were presented with evidence, then they would update their beliefs to match the evidence, but regrettably believers fail to understand what makes up evidence and resort to presenting arguments pointing to the beauty of the universe and its complexity. Similarly, suspending judgement is another quality of the counsellor, and essential if the client is to feel accepted unconditionally. To offer an environment free of judgement allows the client to express themselves freely, overcome social conditioning and outmoded beliefs, it can even prepare the venue for the client to become acquainted with their real self, and explore their reality with fresh eyes. However, the biggest block to this happening is the counsellor who unconsciously communicates disapproval through nonverbal cues or by focusing on session content that stands out in their own mind because of their own biases. An example of this could be the counsellor who appears to suddenly sit up in their chair and nod approvingly when a client says they believe 'all men are aggressive,' and they've considered joining a certain church, that they've considered attending a union rally or taking part in an acupuncture session. It's difficult not to express either approval or disapproval of a client if they push your buttons, but it's the responsibility of every counsellor to become acquainted with their own buttons or triggers and not to be automatically controlled by them like an excited child.

THE DEFAULT POSITION

Atheism has been described as the default position. A baby is born with instincts or innate templates which are the basis of learning, but they're born without beliefs. They do not believe in God, nor have they ever made a judgement regarding anything at all. They exist in the moment. Their innate templates make them cry when they're hungry and sleep and make playful sounds when they're content. From this point they can build on their sounds through interaction, but initially, the sounds they make are meaningless unless it's the sound of discomfort. Apart from their innate templates, babies are a true blank slate which is waiting for experience to write something. They do not believe in a God until someone tells them such a being exists. As part of a child's innate templates, they have pure empathy. If they're held by an adult who is a little nervous, they'll empathically reflect the feeling by sensing the breathing and heartbeat of the adult and burst into tears. If they hear one child cry, they automatically cry for no other reason than they're generating the emotion they witness. Babies are the purest form of humans, before the development of beliefs, values and bias. The baby has no belief in God and is therefore, by definition, an atheist. Let's remember, Atheism is not 'the belief that God doesn't exist,' it's rather just 'the absence of a belief in God.'

The baby also has the quality of congruence or genuineness. If the baby feels pain or is hungry, it does not suppress the emotional discomfort to fit into social acceptability but bellows a scream until needs are met. They don't believe in angels; they don't believe in demons that will harm them, rather they exist in the moment. Existing in the moment is a healthy place to be. In the moment, we do not regret the past or worry about the future. Buddhists attempt to use meditation to exist perfectly in the moment, and counsellors can be seen using similar techniques to calm their mind before entering a counselling session. It's important to be in the moment within the counselling session, to be present in our entirety for the client or we could be perceived as not paying attention and not valuing the client. The default position is also devoid of prejudice. It's human nature to have a preconceived idea of someone's characteristics based on how they look and sound. We see the world through filtered eyes. If someone wears a suit and tie we assume they're worthy of more respect than someone in shorts and a Homer Simpson t-shirt, depicting the cartoon character with his butt crack on display. If we meet a homeless man, we might assume he has an alcohol problem or has mental health problems because of learned stereotypes. If we meet a religious minister, we might assume he is a virtuous person. The list could go on, but these assumptions whether casting the individual in a positive or negative light are prejudiced and based on superficial pieces of information and can lead to further embarrassing inaccuracies. Even the experiences of clients can cause us to make prejudgements about future clients with similar issues or characteristics. A classic form of this is that Anorexic girls are stereotypically believed to have suffered some kind of sexual abuse. A counsellor with this kind of belief may well feel frustrated if the client does not disclose their deep secret, when in-fact this 'assumed secret' does not exist in this client's case at all. The worst kind of prejudice we can experience is the phenomena of over familiarity with a client. Most counsellors enter into training because they're working through some issues themselves and find it useful to learn about their own process as well as being able to receive the support of a classroom which is also full of like-minded people. The wounded healer then embarks on their mission to ease the distress of members of the public who experience the same distress and as a result fail to appreciate the uniqueness of each client's experience and in effect invalidate the client by unintentionally requiring them to fit into the counsellor's idea of their story. The challenge is greater to counsel someone who's experienced similar issues without confusing them with your own. A woman who lost her father in a boating accident seeks bereavement counselling with Linda. Linda became a counsellor because she coincidentally lost her father under similar circumstances. Linda was close to her father and would visit most days with her children. Linda lost her father when he slipped off an inflatable dolphin at Butlins and could not resurface because a rubber ring was stuck to his ankles, keeping him submerged upside down. Linda feels that she is the right counsellor to see this client as she will have the most empathy because of her deeper understanding. When Linda counsels the woman, it becomes apparent to the client that Linda is making too many assumptions about her situation.

Client: I lost my Father in a boating accident two years ago, but I cannot stop thinking about him and our relationship.

Counsellor Linda: You were close to your father and could not come to terms with his death. You long for the relationship you lost and feel you'll never be close to anyone again.

Client: Oh fuck no, I hated the bastard. He used to beat my mother when I was young. Every day she would have bruises. He would never give us any money for clothes or food and would spend all the money on alcohol. He's dead now, and I'm pleased, but I also feel guilty because I sent him a horrible letter before he died, telling him how much I wanted his love but never received it.

Counsellor Linda: Oh.

As we can see Linda had no empathy because she was initially viewing the client's world from her own frame of reference and had failed to establish rapport. This breakdown in a counselling session can happen on a more subtle level, it doesn't have to be a major issue, but it illustrates why being the 'blank slate' is important and we should avoid assumptions. We cannot help but have a certain set of beliefs and values which unintentionally intrude on our counselling practice every now and again, but it's important to keep attention to personal development and identify erroneous ideas. Most computers come with an antivirus program, humans don't have such a luxury for their mind and yet we are bombarded everyday by a vast amount of information, all of which has the potential to distort your entire perception of reality. A baby is ready to assimilate any information. If the baby experiences love and care, then it will learn the world is safe and as a result will experience less stress than the baby who is neglected and harmed. The harmed baby will view the world as a dangerous place and have constant stress and pessimism. From this early start and its degrees of fulfilment and love, the baby learns its worth. A well cared for child will feel loved and secure in any situation that does not involve being eaten by a python. If they criticise the parents cooking, vote for a different political party than the parents, marry someone of the same sex, stop believing in Santa Claus, and they still have their parents love and freely be who they truly are. This child has the best groundwork for growing in self-esteem and experiencing a fulfilled life. Self esteem is a great antivirus program. A person with self esteem will not require the approval of other people to have a sense of self worth. They'll not change their beliefs and values with the view of acceptance by a group or person, unless it's in line with their own reasoning. In Maslow's Hierarchy of Needs, to have security, love and self-esteem are the foundations of Self Actualisation. The abused child finds they crave security and love, but they're sometimes lucky to get food and water. This experience leaves us open to viruses of the mind. Unlike the loved child, the neglected child has to adapt to the demands of their parents to feel safe or experience love. Children who have love rationed by their parents can be conditioned to believe ethnic minorities are subhuman, God exists and demands their loyalty, hate homosexuals and Hell is a place for the disobedient. Add anything you like to this list and a child will absorb it if they fear losing your love. Self esteem is rather like an antivirus for the mind. I'm not talking about pride or arrogance, but a healthy and realistic sense of self compared to others. Someone with self esteem has what's called a strong internal locus of evaluation. An Internal Locus of Evaluation is our own internal system for assessing the world and coming to judgements. The child who needs to adapt to their parents requirements will learn to ignore their own valuing system and become dependent on the judgements of other people and gradually develop low self esteem. The problems of a strong external locus of evaluation are choices of career, life partner and religion will come from someone else. True fulfilment cannot be found except in a reward received for obedience. Their lack of confidence and sense of dependency on people to decide for them makes a person vulnerable to anyone who offers them love and safety for obedience. To tell a child a God made the universe distort their entire perception of reality. In addition, if the child is told 'holy scriptures' are the word of God, then they'll have a large amount of information affecting their perceptions, creating schematic entanglement. This is apparent in the way the Bible is used to infect young minds by Christian fundamentalists in parts of the USA's education system. Teachers are known to use the bible as a science and history book, which cannot not be criticised without social exclusion. These teachers even adapt and pervert scientific findings to support their own worldview and feed this nonsense to their pupils. While this approach is mixed with the threat of rejection by their friends, family and wider community, the tendency to conform both behaviour and thinking can be compelling for an individual with a strong external locus of evaluation. Humans will sacrifice their own desires and ability to think for themselves to maintain their sense of belonging. Children who are taught from infancy to obey or risk rejection or abandonment will probably develop an external locus of evaluation with such strength they'll accept the most ridiculous beliefs as fact into adulthood. This will vary in degree from in each individual depending on the strength of their conditioning during infancy. Adults who accept the world is 6000 years old, flooded with water 2000 years later and selected animals received tickets to sail on a wooden boat to a Turkish mountain. They believe in miracles of faith healing and the virtue of genocide and ethnic cleansing against other minorities when it's their God's command to do so. Biblical tales of atrocities such as rape, sex slavery, paedophilia and the mass murder of children in the Bible committed by their biblical heroes is viewed as justified by its followers by the strange reasoning that God's commands are unquestionably pure. When they're asked why they believe God's commands are unquestionably pure, they'll refer to the evidence found in the Bible. The most common recruiting technique for people of these religions is emotional child abuse with threats of hell-fire and Armageddon. The blank slate cannot differentiate fact from fiction, especially when parents firmly believe it themselves. These beliefs are extreme, common, and not talked about in the open. Seemingly intelligent people are happy to justify the atrocities committed in God's name using reasoning from a bible teacher, such as "It was pure, because it's God's will" or "The people were warned by God's prophet of the consequences of ignoring God's command" and will repeat erroneous reasoning like an obedient parrot in the hope they'll gain direct approval from the Bible. An individual who has suppressed their own empathy in favour of blind ethical guidance from a book or religious teacher has in effect switched off their moral barometer. Empathy is the natural moral compass in life. By examining how their own blank slate was written upon, they come to understand how they became who they are . During this exploration, values and beliefs are identified which may prevent them from conducting therapy. If they do, then they're more able to work toward overcoming programming through personal development exercises. Counsellors will have their own 'shit' to work through and usually it's a bitter-sweet pill of breaking an emotional abscess which allows the wound to heal. Many trainees find the emotional challenge of training too difficult and leave early in their training. Facing all the pain and many humiliations of the past and the examination of one's own inadequacies can be too much to bear, but challenging and changing our perception of reality can be harder to face, not because they're painful, but because our ego and pride are attached to them. We may find instead of a victim of circumstances we are a spoilt bully who demands other people conform to our own requirements. We all want to look in the mirror and see something complimentary, but trainees who expect to look in the mirror and see a 'good person who is suffering' can be distressed to see a bully who is causing suffering to others. Some will leave training when they face their own vulnerabilities and can feel their psychological defences being exposed. Harold had spent most of his life caring for his father and as a result had never pursued a career, education or entered a romantic relationship. He attempted to hide his feelings of vulnerability by presenting a façade of confidence. During his counselling training, he presents an intellectual façade to defend himself. People use defence mechanisms to protect their vulnerabilities and to keep facts out of awareness. Harold's use of internationalisation is one of the most heartbreaking you can witness because the defence wasn't strong enough for the new skills the students were practising and he was experiencing distress and the desire to leave the situation before he lost face. Intellectualise is a defence mechanism allowing an individual to talk about their situation from a distance, as if they're the observer of their own life and of their own feelings and suffering in the same way a philosopher contemplates simple things using long pretentious words. Harold had desperately wanted to fall in love and find a fulfilling career, but his commitment to his dad had prevented this from happening, and he experienced feelings accompanying regret and resentment. He attempted to speak about himself from the third person, and discussed his life as an abstract occurrence, becoming an increasingly philosophical idea of determinism which took attention away from his painful feelings and ownership of his own life.

Howard: There is sometimes a disruption in events one experiences in situations that one will find oneself. you'll need to find a resolution and apply it.

Trainee Counsellor: When you speak about oneself and state 'You', will need to find a resolution, are you talking about yourself or someone else?

Howard: In a disruptive situation we will all need to ponder resolutions, but they're not always apparent to the onlooker.

Trainee Counsellor: I get a sense that you are talking about your own distress and you have felt unable to find a resolution. Would that be right?

Howard: Ah, it's something we all experience, but there's so many resolutions and so many opportunities, but will the price be worth paying?

Howard endured ten minutes in this trainee triad, but the panic evoked by his defence mechanism being challenged was too much and never returned to the classroom. He nearly met himself for the first time, but he didn't feel safe enough to allow this to happen. It must have felt too risky for Harold to take off the defensive mask. He might have felt liberated, but when an individual is buried deep in their masks and defences, it can be painful to face your vulnerabilities without professional support existing beyond a classroom. Not only would people witness his vulnerability, but he would risk losing his sense of dignity. The stronger the defence mechanisms created by the experiences added to our blank slate then the safer we must feel in the therapy room to have them revealed, faced and resolved. Our defences are something we adapt to protect ourselves from the evaluation of onlookers, painful situations, information which challenges accepted reality and hide from aspects of ourselves we find unacceptable, create blocks in awareness and panic when facts are inescapable. These defences can render us neurotic. It would be nice if we could just return our minds to the way they were when we were babies and start again. Unfortunately, putting the damage right is a little more complicated than resetting a smartphone to factory settings. We have to untangle a web of misinformation and the subsequent perceptions and beliefs affected by those pieces of misinformation. The human mind is like a library of uncategorised books where fact and fiction are difficult to distinguish, and at worst the same library where each book gives you a painful electric shock when you attempt to move a book to its rightful section. We all learn by correlating new information to previous learning. If our mind is a library, then every book is a piece of knowledge. When we learn something new, we put a new book on the shelf and run a piece of string from that book to any other book which helps us to understand and relate to the new knowledge. The book with the most pieces of string leading to it will have a dominant effect on how all other pieces of information are understood. If an individual has a good grasp of mathematics, then it's likely they'll be more prepared to understand the sciences and the strings will lead to other branches of science bearing similarities (let's say biology, physics and chemistry). The subject of mathematics is the central tenet of all the sciences and essential for verifying truth. But what if mathematics was proven to be a false teaching? I can use maths, because it's probably the only constant in the universe. If mathematics was proven to be inaccurate, false dogma, then all the knowledge we have acquired which has led to the invention of computers, medical interventions and space exploration have been lucky accidents. Everything we have today results from mathematically dependent science. Our education system would be destroyed as we'd no longer have a means of verifying truth. Instead, every person would be left to believe anything they were told, whether it's regarding God or that the sea is made of tomato soup. Mathematics permeates through scientific theories and as a result science cannot exist without it. Remove mathematics and you remove science. If you likewise remove God from a person's central beliefs, then a similar effect will happen upon their perception of reality. With that in view we can understand why someone would fight to keep hold of a nonsensical belief against the bombardment of reason, to let the belief go would risk the insecurity of emptiness and hopelessness. The human mind needs to feel the security of expectation and hope, even if it's irrational. To live without the comfort blanket of myth requires transcendence and bravery to be patient and accept some things that are unknown. To return to the strings of schematic entanglement, each piece of information we acquire is like a piece of string. We recognise similarities and correlations in new information using our ability to recognise patterns and as the strings of knowledge increase, the greater they become entwined and dependent on each other for consistency. They become entangled, and like the wires behind a TV set, they require effort and emotional fortitude to unravel. We use previous learnings to assist us in understanding new knowledge. If something holds true, it'll affect how we perceive and plan other beliefs. Learning is a process of pattern matching and schematic entanglement as every chunk of learning enables us to better understand the increasingly more complicated information we'll receive, in becoming inseparable and entwined. This is important because without this ability it would be impossible to learn increasingly complicated ideas and skills. Learning maths must first start with basic addition and slowly lead to mathematics which is too baffling for the average mind. Language is also learned in the same way and is probably the best example of schematic entanglement. An individual will learn basic words and associate these words with needs and things that they experience. Those words and their associations can then be transferred and used to express concepts in the hope the listener will understand. When two physics professors enter a debate, it becomes obvious things they can explain in a sentence contain concepts which take years of study to understand. Many ideas such as self actualisation and the collective unconscious can be misunderstood as a spiritual experience if previous learning strings become erroneously correlated to new information. We need to unravel previous experiences to prevent new information being miscategorised in the mind's library. As we go through life, we formulate beliefs about everything whether it's regarding the reliability of buses, the safety of bungee jumping and the intentions of men with ginger beards. Beliefs affect our entire world-view and they're normally resistant to change. It's easier to avoid unravelling the tangled strings to gain an accurate understanding, but rather to hold on to current beliefs dogmatically, this dogmatic approach to life is the reason faith and religion still rule the hearts and minds of its prisoners. Even in the face of evidence, people will hold on to their plainly ridiculous beliefs in favour of the sense of security they provide. This problem is exacerbated when we're part of a community which shares some of those mythical beliefs. The belief is reinforced when we feel we share common knowledge, because more people appear to believe it's more likely to be true, as if truth was a democracy. This gives rise to common sense. Common sense is a belief held by a group rather than created by an individual's own unbiased reasoning. The people of a village sitting at the foot of an erupting volcano fail to evacuate because they reinforce each other's beliefs that the scientist's calculations are wrong. It becomes the culture of the village to ignore the scientific warnings and shake their heads in contempt at their 'would be rescuers'. Erroneous beliefs appear credible to most humans because of the tendency of confirmation bias. Confirmation bias is a characteristic of exclusively noticing evidence which reinforces existing beliefs, while ignoring anything to the contrary. Bill believes female drivers are clumsy and dangerous on the road. As soon as he sees a woman behind the wheel of a car, his adrenaline pumps around his veins and he is ready to pull on his brakes to avoid a collision. He drives past a crash on the road and looks for the woman who caused it. He sees a car parked across two spaces; he believes it was a woman who parked the offending vehicle. If he crashes into the back of a woman's car, then it was her fault for slamming on the brakes. If the same woman crashes into the back of his car, then it was also her fault for not paying attention. His 'confirmation bias' is preventing him from seeing the truth or making any sound judgement. His view of reality is nothing more than a product of his programming. We can extend these beliefs to race and religion, even about science and reality. It appears there's no real wisdom in holding a rigid belief which is not open to change. Without openness to change or the willingness to be open minded, there can be no approach to understanding truth. Resistance to change is called the 'Conservative impulse'. Preserving our own rigid view of reality in the face of mounting evidence is a painful experience. Anyone who has found evidence their spouse has been cheating on them knows ignoring the evidence or attributing it to something else to avoid emotional pain. When a family member dies we experience extreme distress as the change cannot be hidden from awareness due to the cruel evidence continuously reminding you they're no longer here and they are not coming back. When a family member or close friend dies we find our sense of security is disrupted. Feelings of abandonment and loneliness can lead to despair. Maslow placed security at the second level of the hierarchy of needs, security comes from love and belonging affecting our self concept and self esteem directly. The conservative impulse exists despite the evidence to protect our fragile reality within our short existence. All the above issues are presented to counsellors and psychotherapists regularly, loss and bereavement, relationship problems, and anger issues always appear to have some Conservative impulse preventing change the view of reality and the acceptance of a fresh vision. Advice on how to view women, how to view adultery and bereavement are among a vast array of beliefs pre-packaged by religion for its followers to absorb. Our own reason and common sense are not always good guides to truth. We are always influenced by bias and conditioned thinking. Our cultural beliefs can be classified as common sense in our own cultural setting, but when we enter another culture, we may appear eccentric. When my youngest son was 3 years old, he witnessed two Buddhist monks shopping in Ikea for candles. He immediately realised their dress was different to the rest of the people he would encounter from day to day and with indignation of a middle-aged bigot, shouted at the top of his voice, "What are they doing here." It appears we humans also have a tendency to reject anything challenging our perception of what's 'normal'. I may well be understating the human reaction to differences in culture and perception. Humans will reject, destroy other cultures, with murder, ethnic cleansing or covert 'integration into society.' The suspicion and fear of anything appearing to contradict accepted cultural perceptions regarding common sense is seen as logical, and this fear exists in every human unless they've acknowledged their bias and transcended their cultural programming. Cultural programming feels like truth. It's referred to as common sense. It comes from dogmatic introjects which are our fundamental beliefs regarding reality. It's difficult to identify the folly of our dogmatic introjects as they're reinforced by our social environment such as family and friends. It's when we leave such environments and enter situations or cultures where we appear eccentric and are forced to question the validity of our fundamental beliefs. An example of this can be found in Marissa who grew up in a strong Christian family. Marissa was taught from an early age that God created the earth and all life on it according to the Bible's account. She was told scientists had misled the world with satanic teachings of evolution. She was told anyone outside her church should be viewed with suspicion because they're influenced by the devil. When she leaves home to start university she needs to associate with other students and finds they don't behave immorally or depraved. In fact, Marissa finds many of the people she meets to have good moral values, even though they do not attend her church. As she studies for her university degree, she encounters a true presentation of science without the interpretation of her church and finds it to be logical. The difficulty Marissa's dogmatic introjects have now been challenged and she may have to re-evaluate her entire view of reality. This is not a small thing to experience, it represents a crisis to anyone who experiences it and involves an actual experience of bereavement as our old vision of reality, our God dies and the perception of family is altered to something feeling uncomfortable. Changing one's view of reality is always anxiety provoking. Existential therapy is adopted to address these problems as an individual can truly feel lost and meaningless in such situations and will need to come to terms with a new view of reality where meaning and purpose are not as universal and straightforward as we have been led to believe. Having a sense of purpose and meaning contributes toward a sense of security and to have this taken away without the time to accommodate the changes can cause serious anxiety. To be fair, if Marissa's anxiety was too great, she would probably leave university and return home. It would be the most painless option. She found comfort in the myths of her culture and died happy but ignorant of facts. Most people do not have the courage to face uncertainty, they would much rather embrace a folly where there's love and acceptance as a reward rather than risk walking the undiscovered country offering development toward truth based on facts. People become anxious when they're presented with evidence contradicting a current view of reality, but there's also the actual threat they can become violently enraged and behave in a downright 'bonkers way' by such revelations. The churches invented the crime of heresy to prevent any deviation from accepted understanding, and they persecuted anyone who might fancy their chances of 'thinking critically' by burning a few of them for good measure. Fortunately, times have changed and the anxiety the churches feel nowadays can only be quelled by promising the compassionate God will burn the bastards in hell for all eternity for contradicting his nonsensical bollocks. If you don't believe me check out some heated debates, we find as Christians and scientists debate the biblical age of the universe as being 7000 years old. The argument between scientists and Christian leaders is the universe either came here through scientific processes, or we appeared because God fancied some worship. Well, we all have days like that, don't we? The problem of how we 'know what we know' is not questioned by the masses. We find it difficult to accept change and enter a grieving process for any loss whether it's a bereavement, loss of a career or financial loss until we can accommodate our new circumstances. The more dogmatic our thinking and our view on reality then the less likely it is we'll recover from grief without some form of psychotherapeutic intervention. We avoid any challenge to our established knowledge, it's painful and we long for the peace and comfort of any old knowledge supplies. We know what we know, and anyone who contradicts this comforting fact is a troublemaker who needs to shut their diversion face before people gasp in indignation. Religion has used its power of providing meaning to people, with the result they control people's lives from birth to death. It has controlled their decisions, finances and political decisions. It's hard to find a government in the world that has not gained influence without expressing a religious affiliation. Being part of a religious culture provides a sense of camaraderie and a sense of direction and safety, whether it's right or wrong. Being accepted as part of the norm has helped many leaders gain influence whether these leaders are good or bad. Most times the leaders are poor and motivated by selfish desires to dominate and exploit. Good leaders who can offer support and advancement to their followers may well be rejected by their culture if their message deviates and threatens the established truth. In the far flung past we find critical thinkers, scientists and philosophers who suggested our cherished knowledge might be wrong and a more complicated and fascinating reality was waiting to be discovered. These well-meaning trouble makers were promptly 'shut up' by the 'powers that be' by literally shutting them up in a cell or perhaps executing them. This brought comfort to many. It meant the masses could feel safe in the knowledge they would be resurrected after death, God loves them, and their suffering will be over when they're reunited in heaven with their loved ones. The evidence of the scientific thinkers brought uncertainty, and the prospect of not knowing what the future will bring after death. It also risked the despair accompanying a belief that life could be a meaningless journey ending in oblivion. The scientists haven't brought a message; rather they've presented us with facts, which have been harnessed to the benefit of mankind. Scientists have brought us medicines preventing disease and invented technologies that made travel and education accessible. Some would argue knowledge has been applied in horrific ways, but the scientist's purpose was to find and present the facts. If the facts contradict existing beliefs they're not obliged to provide a replacement belief, rather they'll provide the unsatisfactory, but true answer of "we don't have the answer to that question yet". It's a general rule, humans don't tolerate ambiguity well, and they can't allow a gap in their knowledge from existing without filling it with something, and that something is usually a God. If a human's present belief in God is inconsistent with reality, they instead change their God into something different so he can still exist in a world where knowledge is slowly extinguishing the great being into oblivion as the void of ignorance is filled. People may use religion as a quick fix while they get on with their lives, not giving their beliefs much thought compared to fact. We don't all have time to think about the 'Big Bang,' 'evolution by natural selection' or even how many calories are in a pork pie. It was, and still is, an argument between the giants of reason and the well-educated theologians. Generally, humans don't like to be proven wrong. We get embarrassed, humiliated and various other synonyms which refer to our red faced, ego damaged addiction to groundless pride. As a result of this charming characteristic, we avoid any knowledge requiring a rethink about everything classified as truth. In 1957 the BBC broadcast a Panorama program educating people about how Spaghetti is grown and harvested from trees. This was an April fool's joke, but many of the British public believed this was a true story and continued to believe it despite the evidence to the contrary. The reason for their rigid belief in the spaghetti tree was nothing other than that they trusted the BBC as a reliable source of information. Even after being taken to an Italian restaurant to watch spaghetti being made with flour and egg, they were still doubtful the BBC would report something false. Fortunately, the poor fooled public didn't have access to YouTube to provide counter evidence by replaying the practical joke as a reference to truth. Of course, watching spaghetti being made in the flesh is a lot more convincing than a BBC broadcast, but some people trust the BBC before they trust their eyes. The BBC was making a harmless joke, but the media has been used in some countries to spread propaganda and lies. A glance through the satellite channels will present religious channels which promote their own beliefs and supply inspiring stories of healing and to rally support for their financial aims. If we can be fooled by the media having a bit of fun, how much more can people be fooled by a trusted religion using a trusted holy book? I was approached by a couple of well meaning Christian preachers who were hoping to save me from the wrath of their loving God. Referring to their holy book, they presented good reasoning regarding knowledge, which was spouted from their mouths like 'well trained parrots that have absolutely no idea how to apply such a useful maxim'. They stated, "If you were on a journey, and someone showed you on a map you are on the wrong road, would you take their advice and continue on your wrong course?" I answered, "If the map was a 2000 year old copy, would you follow the bloody thing?" They thought for a while and realized, rightfully, I wasn't as receptive to their well-meaning bullshit as my angelic face might suggest. Maps are brilliant guides to get you somewhere as long as it's a recent one. I went to Yorkshire and many of the roads and villages in my 1975 copy of the AA Road Book are now in the sea because of coastal erosion. I suppose the Christian preachers would've just driven into the sea. Then again, perhaps not. They would probably blame it on the sin of the people who dwelt in those settlements. They were probably disobeying God by relaxing during their retirement, getting involved in sexual monstrosities and playing bingo too regularly at the local community centre, which ironically, is still standing to this day on a precipice. Anyway, the point they made was a good one, even though they hadn't a clue how to apply it in their own life. "If you were on a journey and someone showed you on a map you're on the wrong road, would you still continue the same way?" My answer is, "Is the map trustworthy and up to date?" I might trust the kind soul with a map and arrive at my destination to find it has sunk into the freezing North Sea. I will now have evidence the map is a tad wrong, but it won't help me or the poor retired Bingo Players who committed sexual monstrosities before God just blighted them. We can only trust evidence. I'm not talking about anecdotal evidence, where someone tells you a story about how they were brought back from the dead by the power of prayer or the story of how someone was abducted by sex starved aliens, or even the story of a witness who has seen from their own eyes that spaghetti grows on trees. No, they're adding the ingredients of fantasy to the story. I'm talking about verifiable evidence, the stuff that'd be acceptable in court, supported by facts. Here's one of the most influential psychotic episodes which stands as an example of faith for the most morally confused religions of the world. Genesis 22 states: *Sometime later, God tested*

Abraham's faith. "Abraham!" God called. "Yes," he replied. "Here I am." "Take your son, your only son—yes, Isaac, whom you love so much—and go to the land of Moriah. Go and sacrifice him as a burnt offering on one of the mountains, which I will show you."... When they arrived at the place where God told him to go, Abraham built an altar and arranged the wood on it. Then he tied his son, Isaac, and laid him on the altar on top of the wood. Abraham picked up the knife to kill his son as a sacrifice.

If you cherish your deeply held beliefs and hold them dogmatically while doing silly things it would be reasonable, although not diplomatic, to say, "you're deluded." It's not because I don't respect religion or dogmatic beliefs, I respect these things. I respect them in the same way I respect a contagious disease or a vicious animal. They're damaging, dangerous and should be approached with caution. There's no virtue in defending something harmful.

Everything we learn as a child is accepted as truth because critical thinking is not fully developed. This is initially helpful to a child. Humans would've died out a long time ago if children tested a parent's assertion that picking up snakes is a bad idea or eating certain mushrooms will kill you. Natural selection has provided children with the tendency to believe everything they're told to protect them from death and live to pass on their genes to future generations. The side effect of such a tendency is to accept erroneous information as fact. The belief in God is a powerful belief when combined with organised religious rules and consequences. The child is told they'll burn in hell for all eternity if they disobey God. Children must marry a God-fearing spouse, obey authority, be humble and experience shame about their sexual feelings as they develop and view with suspicion anyone who is not part of their religious persuasion. The child starts life with a set of innate drives and instincts. These innate templates are the foundation of all knowledge and will develop based on experience and guidance from others. All knowledge becomes a filter to perception which is used to expand understanding of the world by applying a hypothesis to new experiences. One piece of learning will contribute to future understanding of the world and will also be involved in reaching conclusions about our complete reality. If I am told snakes are harmful, this will mean I fear snakes, however I may see a similarity in other animals and generalise this avoidance to include worms, newts and lizards. Pet shops, ponds and gardens could all become places where these animals could appear. As a child experiences these animals and their knowledge increases, they can have a more accurate view of the dangers, and the creatures are no longer categorized in the child's mind as being similar or dangerous. A child might see a friend become ill after eating a poisonous berry from a bush. The child may well avoid any fruit growing from a bush and extend it to all fruit, but after a while, after seeing evidence of people eating blackberries and apples with no ill effects, they'll probably start eating fruit again. These experiences appear to have unnecessary consequences on perception of reality, but the web of deceptive experiences is usually untangled with a dose of convincing evidence. Erroneous beliefs permeate our mind and affect all aspects of our learning and perceptions. For example, the belief men are superior to women affected by western society resulting in women unable to gain senior positions in companies or find employment at all in stereotypically male roles. The reasons women experience discrimination are probably something originating from our far-flung past. If you look in ancient literature like the Bible you can see women were prevented from holding a senior position because of tradition, so this is not a new problem (1 Timothy 2:12). Rules of what was appropriate and inappropriate surrounded women. My Grandma's tea parties were a good example of discrimination. She would have a large plate of cakes for the family every time we visited. If there was one cake left, she insisted that it should go to one of the men. My female cousins couldn't understand why the boys were given priority, but this was a deep seated value from the days when men worked down mines and were the breadwinner. In my Grandma's mind, this was an important value. Children are born with an innate tendency to investigate the world around them. They're like scientists reaching out to their spinning mobiles, rotating above their cot. They bring objects to their mouth and test what can be manipulated and what tastes good. I remember all three of my sons would sit in their playpen with their toys but would constantly look for ways to escape. My youngest son worked out early, he could use his toys as steps and climb out. His ability to do this wasn't an innate ability to create steps, but it was down to his innate ability to learn as he explored his environment. His mind could make connections, see patterns as he played and learned. Eventually two or more ideas came together to give him inspiration, insight, or a hypothesis on how to escape the confines of the playpen. He tested his hypothesis and found it was an effective way to escape his captivity.

Ug the hunter, gatherer finds a Beehive and discovers he can extract honey from it. He develops a hypothesis. His hypothesis is that all insect colonies will produce honey to feed themselves. He comes across an ants nest and is excited to extract the honey. He tears the nest apart, but discovers no honey. He gets covered in angry ants. They all bit him. He runs to the nearby lake screaming and dives in to wash all the ants off his now itchy body. The great hunter gatherer called Ug discovered his hypothesis was wrong and realises not all insect colonies will provide honey. He must now re-test his hypothesis and decide beehives are the most likely place to find honey. It's the human tendency to test things and formulate beliefs based on their experience. The human mind contains both instincts and programming. Experience in life contributes to our programming and determines all beliefs about the world. Belief systems affect the perception of everything. Whether it's based on experience, philosophy or religious training, you can't help having your world-view affected by beliefs. Our beliefs affect our preferences, acting as the director of bias and discrimination; A Christian who meets a homosexual may be reminded of God's wrath on Sodom and Gomorrah, if you believe anyone who is Asian is also a 'fundamentalist Muslim fanatic' then you may have a dim view of any Hindu, Sikh or Buddhist. You will have a generalized view of Islam, based on nothing but news reports. If you believe in a God who'll torture you for eternity for eating a bacon sandwich, using his name in vain or even farting in a lift, then you'll probably apply the same valuing system to other people you meet and view them as worthy of eternal punishment if they commit any of those sins. Beliefs can bring about happy biases. If you believe everyone has a good side, then you can encourage everyone to grow and flourish. Wherever they come from, they're powerful and will affect our complete view of the universe and the people in it. I'm not saying this is a bad thing; it's just this is how we create a map of reality in our minds. Beliefs are a group of biases determining our perceptions. Humans have a predisposition to form beliefs and hold on to them as a secure guide to their life, to transcend such an instinctive trait would bring us closer to reality, but could also take away a sense of certainty humans desire as part of their innate need for safety.

Atheism is the absence of a belief, rather than a belief system. You could suggest that it would mean an absence of a mind virus, but beliefs include any true or false information. Specifically, Atheism is the absence of a belief in a God or Gods, it's not however the assertion there is no God, just the absence of the belief. *"Saying atheism is a belief system is like saying not going skiing is a hobby. I've never been skiing. It's my biggest hobby. I literally do it all the time." ~Ricky Gervais.* Saying "I don't believe in God" is not the same as stating "God does not exist." Atheism is represented by society as a belief system, but this is wrong. The definition of the word 'atheist' refers to what's 'not believed.' It's natural they would place atheism into that group of religious categories in a world indoctrinating children from birth. Perhaps people are confused by the suffix 'ISM' which is normally attached to a religion or group holding specific ideals. Buddhism, Sikhism, communism, capitalism and Catholicism are all known for their ideals distinguishing them from each other. People in the world who do not believe in God may still hold a belief in something supernatural such as spirits or the disembodied human soul. The Atheism I am discussing goes beyond an absence of belief in a God and includes an absence of belief in any supernatural or spiritual assertion that cannot be tested objectively. Richard Dawkins explains the extension of his atheism to anything supernatural by stating "I am also an A-faryist". Atheism will normally mean an individual does not have a religion but because Buddhists don't follow a God and are therefore atheist in the strict definition of the word, however it's true Buddhists have a belief in the soul and

Karma and will refer to their belief system as Non-theist, rather than atheist. This is not true of all Buddhists. A minority don't believe in Karma or reincarnation following Buddha's teaching as a secular philosophy. The Atheism I am discussing in this book is 'informed and scientific Atheism.' With this perspective it can be explained that Atheism is not a belief system but a conclusion based on evidence. This perspective requires the individual to have a mindset using 'critical thinking' and a non bias perspective. This thinking is not averse to contradictory evidence, but it's open to change if experience contradicts existing beliefs regarding the world. This is a flexible/non-dogmatic approach to reality where the individual avoids thinking in absolutes. Human babies are born without beliefs. They're, in effect, born atheists; it's the 'default position' of every human. Every child born into this world does neither believe in God, the tooth fairy or Santa Claus, but they learn this belief through education from parents. Atheism is the default position because it's our original and pure outlook because there's an absence of beliefs. Human infants are also the most uninhibited and honest people you'll find on the planet. They're at their most congruent, genuine and authentic at this stage of their lives, and their guide is their instincts. A child cries because this is their instinctual reaction to the experience of discomfort, but there is no expectation or belief that anyone will tend to their needs until this is reinforced by the regular loving response of their caregivers. The belief mother will eventually arrive to attend to their needs is reinforced by witnessing the continuous reliability of the mothers' attendance when the child cries. The child has no belief milk will take away the sensation of hunger until they experience it. The child develops beliefs through experience and experimentation. The benefit of speech is the ability to learn from other people's experience and reasoning without the need to experiment yourself. Infant humans will accept anything said to them, such as the tooth fairy leaves money for teeth. What's more important, the human infant has no self concept. It neither thinks of itself in degrees of bad or good, clever or stupid, Christian or Hindu, working class or middle class, there's only experience. Their self concept is developed as they grow older through experience and verbal explanations. If a child is told they're clever, then they'll have a bias to recognize these traits in themselves and reinforce their belief. If a child is told they're clumsy, inferior because of their race. If they're told they're evil or a deviant because they experience feelings or desires in opposition to religious standards then it's likely they'll become anxious when these experiences manifest themselves. Their self esteem will be lowered and result in their unhappiness in life will be increased while their behaviour and thinking is continuously being adjusted to conform to social/ family/ society requirements. The more dogmatically applied the rules regarding self worth then the more neurotic an individual will become. Atheism does not guarantee an individual will not grow to be neurotic, even an atheist can be filled with neurotic self doubt induced by parents who over push a child to study science instead of exploiting the child's natural talent and desire to follow a career in sport or the arts. The dogmatic indoctrination of children to think in a certain way or to follow certain behaviour is damaging. As a child we patiently absorb knowledge through experience and develop questions as we grow, such as 'where did I come from? What happens when we die? And how was I made?' The answers to these questions might be valid or nonsense, the child knows no difference, they just trust the answers they're given. A baby is ready to become anything you want it to be, but be warned, if the information condemns natural thinking and growth tendencies then the child will develop anxiety when faced with contradictory experience. A natural atheist is a blank slate without a belief system or ego ideal. The infant atheist mind is organismic and guided by the natural actualizing tendency with genuine expressions of emotion, empathy and action. Terms such as Ego ideal, actualizing tendency and organismic are unusual but are common terms in humanistic counselling and knowledge of their process is essential if an individual is to reach their potential and maintain or regain happiness. It needs to be emphasized there's a difference between the 'infant atheist' and the 'Adult atheist'. The adult atheist is not a blank slate and can be as full of prejudice and nonsense as a religionist. The modern Atheist is guided by 'critical thought' and requires beliefs regarding reality to exist as a 'testable hypothesis' which are open to change on the presentation of evidence, rather than to hold on to beliefs as if they're in a 'monkey trap.' Therapists need to take a similar perspective if they're to be effective in creating a therapeutic environment. A counsellor will reject a client who lives in opposition to their cherished dogmatic beliefs. So counsellors must continuously embark on personal development programs, so they can recognize any trait that could damage the therapeutic relationship

Dogmatic thinking is understanding the world through bias and is resistant to change to knowledge. These pieces of knowledge are 'dogmatic introjects' which contribute to a rigid view of the world based on what's absorbed socially through family and religious or philosophical training in life. The belief that all doctors are caring will be resistant to change when the papers report a story about a doctor being found guilty of killing his patients. Instead of condemning the doctor, the dogmatic mind will create excuses for the doctor such as "the doctor was being compassionate in practising euthanasia." This was an actual event when Dr Harold Shipman was found to have killed hundreds of his patients by administering an overdose of morphine. The event sparked a debate in the UK regarding euthanasia and many people sang Dr Shipman's praises for being a principled and compassionate doctor until it was revealed many of his victims were relatively healthy and lead happy lives with their families until he took it upon himself to choose who'd live and who would die. The accusations Priests abused children throughout the world were condemned as an outright lie and attributed to nothing more than an overreaction or a method of gaining compensation for the victims. Dogmatic thinking also applies to other facts we deny in the face of evidence. An example of this is the trend to deny the world is becoming warmer because of carbon emissions. Even though the evidence has proven this is an actual effect contributing to the drastic reduction of polar ice which has made the north west passage available as a trade route; or the tendency of many to believe evolution has no evidence, despite the conclusive proof being abundantly available. Dogmatic thinking is a long and complex subject which causes much grief to its sufferers. People who experience extreme anxiety because they cannot adapt their view of people and reality according to their experiences will visit counsellors. A woman who experiences emotional and physical abuse from her husband can dismiss the evidence presented in every insult and assault. In this way she can maintain respect and admiration for her husband. She holds onto the belief her husband is 'wonderful' and she accepts responsibility for his abusive actions. The counsellor may well listen to the woman discuss how she would like to identify within herself, what exactly she needs to do to please her husband and prevent further punishment, but her dogmatic belief may prevent her from realizing the fact she is a victim of domestic abuse and the desire to change her personality to please her husband expresses low self esteem. It's difficult for someone with low self esteem to think critically. This is usually because they've an 'external locus of evaluation' or they do not trust their own ability to judge a situation and feel dependent on others for guidance. Children rely on their parents for guidance, but this does not mean they've low self esteem. Low self esteem occurs when we develop a self-concept of helplessness and gradually suppress our own valuing system, but even our own self-concept can be a dogmatic introject, and this can be the most difficult schema to change. Domestic abuse is a form of bullying where one partner makes sure the other feels inferior by a constant barrage of threats and requirements. This can be seen in religious parents who demand their children believe in a certain set of spiritual beliefs. The threat of hell fire and the existence of demons is a true reality for the child's mind who trusts everything a parent tells them. For them there's no difference in the statement, "it's dangerous to play in a busy street" and the statement" you'll burn for eternity in hell if you disobey God." Both statements are given by parents who truly believe these concepts are true, but to the child they're indistinguishable. But take this idea further. In order for a child to stay in their parent's religion, the threat of eternal torment is not enough. Perhaps, as a result of their thinking, they'll lose interest in their parents' religion and eventually abandon those archaic beliefs altogether. For a parent who truly believes their child will burn in Hell for not following their particular brand of religion, then the threat is real. The method for making sure a child believes nonsense in the face of fact is to take away their ability to think critically by teaching them to value the virtues of humility, by rejecting man made philosophies and exclusively following the direction of their holy book and the preachers who endorse it. The punishment of disobedience is the anger of your parents and perhaps a physical beating. The fires of Hell are not required at this point. The Atheist will present the scientific method as a means of developing and confirming their own beliefs. They'll also use critical thinking to make sure they're not accepting outright falsehoods as reality. This approach to reality means an individual can suspend judgement until they're satisfied there's enough reason to accept a certain viewpoint. This sounds time consuming, but there's no rush to believe something, even if the person is telling you sincerely and believes 'Armageddon could come.' This approach means you're also willing to change your view of reality as new information is acquired. Theism is different. It starts with a belief in God and attempts to interpret reality and morality based on that belief. Sometimes a belief in a God and certain moral principles is not enough and reality is also understood starting from a holy book written in the Bronze Age such as the bible. This can be problematic for the believer, as the information within holy books can demand 100% devotion while carrying the threat of abandonment from community and family and eternal suffering. Given this kind of pressure, it's not surprising religion appears in psychotherapy sessions as a somewhat pathological presentation, which can take therapists by surprise if they've not encountered indoctrination before. Indoctrination is powerful as it's usually done to a child who has no other experience to contradict what's proclaimed to be true. Families, churches and sadly schools all take part in this practice and contribute to control the fully grown adults' thoughts, feelings and life. It's programming determining all aspects of an individual's experience and perceptions. It can condition people to think and feel in a certain way, and although many religions condemn the use of hypnosis and brainwashing, it's surprising to find in their ignorance this is exactly what they're doing to their members. Any deviation from the 'rules of faith' automatically results in the experience of anxiety, guilt and the need to pray for strength. This suffering is debilitating for too many, who fight with low self esteem as they condemn themselves for falling in love with someone of a different faith or because they would like to escape an abusive marriage. There're many things religion demands of people that appear ridiculous. At a volunteer counselling charity, a Jewish rabbi came to meet us to join our group of volunteers. He politely shook our hands in greeting but refused to shake the hand of the woman in our group because she could be menstruating and this would render him ceremonially unclean. This was ignored, and no fuss was made, but in a vocation where both men and women are equals it would be ridiculous to think such religiously inspired behaviour could have a therapeutic effect. To behave in such a way with a client could be interpreted as a rejection. An individual who wants to think and behave a certain way, but is conditioned by religion to follow dogma, suffers incongruity and the accompanying anxiety. The stronger the dogma then the closer the more isolated the religious community becomes, as this is the place they can feel normal and maintain a sense of self acceptance. Counsellors and psychotherapists work with suffering in its many forms. Suffering is the norm for humans and it's a great motivating factor in our lives. It doesn't matter who we are, we'll all experience suffering, unsatisfactoriness, and we spend most of our lives attempting to avoid it at all costs. We spend much of our time fighting the pain of hunger as we search for food and water and work to maintain some shelter. If we don't have access to fulfil our needs, then we instinctively know illness and death draw closer to us. In western civilization with its abundance, this viewpoint may appear over the top or even irrelevant to think that way, but we do spend most of the time earning money to avoid suffering and to distract ourselves from the apparent futility of living. We're so comfortable in this part of the world that even the poor have TV sets and microwave ovens, but we still suffer and have anxieties such as health problems, money worries and unsatisfactoriness with life as we crave more and more. It's not unusual to find people who have enough finances to see them into old age, who also lose sleep over their career status or if their friends have forgotten to invite them for a game of golf. Like the poorest people on earth, financially wealthy individuals must face the pain of loss as they see loved ones come to the end of their lives. This is a fact of existence. As humans grow old, they watch their children grow and their grandchildren being born. They have the sadness of watching friends die one by one and wondering when their turn will be. Humans know their children will experience death, and in a few generations no one will remember their name. We have no evidence to suggest there's anything more to this life and although many offer their personal experiences as evidence, this evidence is no more substantial than the schizophrenic who is convinced he sees vampires or the fantasist who believes he's a messiah. Memories of fiction and comforting lies are powerful to the listener and reinforce the storyteller's belief in the experience, but that's all. Finding truth is difficult. If someone told you there was treasure buried in the garden, you could prove it's there by finding it; but if you don't find it, then perhaps you need to keep searching. If you were dying of thirst and were told by a kind looking gentleman there's water under the soil, then you might search for it until you die or until you become too weak to continue. For many, God is like that. The promise that there's a powerful father who'll help you is comforting and seductive. Like the treasure in the garden, you cannot prove God is not there. Using the 'you can't disprove it' perspective could prove anything. "You can't prove Darth Vader doesn't exist, therefore he does!" It would be difficult to prove the non-existence of Darth Vader, that George Lucas is a prophet of The Force, just as it's difficult to disprove flying horses and vampires and ghosts. You can search forever looking for something that's not there, but if we truly believe it's there, then we'll not need to find it, we can relax and say with full conviction, "I believe I have found God, because he revealed himself to me." As Oscar Wilde Stated "Religion is like a blind man looking in a black room for a black cat which isn't there, and finding it." This sounds like an unkind thing to say about religion, but it's more a statement about our desire to hide from reality and truth as it reveals itself through science. The need for religion and our tendency to believe without evidence and mould an entire life around a belief in God is more pathological than the black cat which isn't there, because a black cat won't tell you to hate other religions, or believe family members will be eternally punished for not following the rules of the black cat. The black cat would not ask you to demean women, to shun members of your family who are homosexual or feel guilty for having natural sexual feelings. The black cat won't tell you to avoid eating certain foods or teach you certain races are evil. The black cat is just a fiction the blind man claimed he found. The belief in God is more dangerous than the belief in a black cat. Belief in God persuades people to behave and believe certain things to where they'll even kill or sacrifice their lives or the life of their children for the reward of his approval and people are venerated for doing so. All humans are blind to the hidden truths of the universe, and we crave someone to care for us in the same way we were cared for as children. To have a loving father or mother is a genuine comfort to a child. With a loving parent, we can always feel protected. When we find God or religion we feel comforted similarly, but the parent in such a case exists exclusively in the mind. It's nice to believe there's no evidence to dispute it, but to believe in this way is a little embarrassing, unless you're in the company of other people who also entertain similar beliefs. A community of believers can make any belief acceptable and credible within their own group, and to a great extent comfort is derived from the collective delusion. When we believe we have found God, we're emotionally cushioned from the experience of permanent loss as the loss is not perceived as permanent. Our parents and our children have the assurance of reuniting in heaven or in some other form. It goes a long way to reducing suffering and despair, just to believe. It feels better to live in the comfort of ignorance than face the reality of oblivion. In the movie 'Matrix' it's discovered all humans are living in a computer generated world which is controlled by machines. When they're removed from the Matrix world they find they're living in an apocalyptic scene of unpleasantness. While watching the film I couldn't help thinking, for the 100 years or so of life a human gets, it would probably be better to live in the false world, even if it was just for a short break to escape the realities of suffering. Escapism is something we all practice through a good film or book to get away from the reality of life. Many people want the false reality to be the real one at all times and insist their religion is truth and their God is real, and they'll fight to maintain the illusion in their own mind by offering creative metaphors and moving anecdotes of revelations and miracles. Reducing the impact of suffering is something religion, spirituality and a belief in God accomplishes, if it makes people feel better, it's a good thing. This comfort comes at substantial cost to the human need of self determination. Normally the prerequisite for receiving the promised benefits of religion is such as eternal life is to obey certain rules, and this is where suffering begins again in a different form. The rules religion asks people to follow are designed to ensure loyalty and conformity. Comfort is given in exchange for subjugation and dulling of moral conscience. The consequences of disobedience are usually the promise of death, eternal torture or no hope of a resurrection after death. Christians are told in their Bible, "The truth shall set you free," but it appears the minds of the most loyal Christians are captive to the threat of eternal punishment and the dread of losing the promise of eternal life. *"The moment you declare a set of ideas to be immune from criticism, satire, derision and contempt, freedom of thought becomes impossible." —Salman*

Rushdie. The acquisition of truth and knowledge has been the goal of philosophers since the beginning of civilization. The difficulty with philosophy is that some have used their present understanding, beliefs and biases to offer explanations through pondering and speculation, offering no facts. Other philosophers formulated experiments to provide evidence and contributed a new understanding about the world. Both these types of philosophers have followers and like most followers they tend to stick to the thinking they're comfortable with. Ancient man struggled to survive and contribute toward his society. Humans noticed the cycle of life and death and rebirth in nature. He noticed this because his life depended on it. He learned that when crops die, seeds bring new crops the year after. Animals will die, but they can create more life from their offspring than they possess themselves. Humans may die, but the population continues to grow. Life and death were important aspects which require an explanation. Magnificent monuments were built to map out the seasons using the sun, stars and moon to plan when to plant crops and when to reap them; to identify the seasons. Many more questions than he could answer in a lifetime. All humans have dreams while they sleep, ancient people were transported to another world as they slept, some dreams being happy and some dreams frightening. No doubt some more intelligent people, the ones who designed the great celestial temples such as Stonehenge and learned to control fire and extract metals from rocks, would ponder the great questions and offer an idea, perhaps based on their observations of the world's cycles and mysterious dreams and create a spiritual world where the dead find rebirth. It's seductive in the same way alcohol is seductive to the anxious. It's not a real solution, but it distracts us from the pain of reality. Some research suggests people who have religion are among the happiest. If this is true, then the reasons for this should be investigated. If we're dying of thirst, we'll feel happier if we're told the Red Cross are on their way to help. Even if the Red Cross isn't aware of our predicament, the individuals who believe they're coming will feel better, of this there can be no doubt. Religion can also tell us we're valuable in God's sight, which can raise our self esteem. If an individual feels valuable they'll also have self esteem, especially if they believe God loves them so much he sacrificed his own son to save them. A religion also offers a community of like-minded people who reinforce these beliefs to top each other's mutual benefit. In a social world where everyone believes in God and rewards each other for obeying his commands, it's not surprising people feel secure and happy. Although it feels good, there's no reason or evidence to support any of these happy assertions, and without evidence the experience of happiness is based on collective delusion. There could be some wisdom in the words of Slartibartfast 'I'd much rather be happy than right any day,' penned by Douglas Adams in the Hitchhiker's guide to the galaxy. In the hitchhiker's guide to the galaxy Arthur Dent is trying to make sense of his existence and suggests to Slartibartfast there could be intelligence outside the universe we know controlling everything. Slartibartfast offers some wisdom to his question, he states, "Perhaps I'm old and tired, but I think the chances of finding out what's actually going on are so absurdly remote that the only thing to do is to say, "Hang the sense of it," and keep yourself busy. I'd much rather be happy than right any day." This may sound flippant or even derogatory to many people who believe, but if we face a reality contradicting our beliefs, will we have the bravery and humility to alter them, or the wisdom to say "I really don't understand, hang the sense of it"? Is there a greater view of reality that could offer happiness and peace of mind? Happiness and peace based on reality will stand the test of time better than happiness based on fantasy. A fantasy becomes a lie when it's presented as a fact, and a lie must be reinforced by distortion of truth if it's maintaining believers. Humans can be seen to distort and suppress reality in counselling all the time. People come to counselling because they're usually having difficulty in adapting to some aspect of the real world which cannot be hidden. One woman had difficulty accepting her son was gay and planning a transgender operation. She was referred for counselling by her doctor. Her distortion and suppression of reality was manifest when she said, "He wasn't always gay, you know. When he was sixteen, he liked girls. He liked them so much he would dress up in his sister's clothes and pretend to be one!" For an individual to have a comfortable relationship with reality, there must be a congruence between belief and experience. In other words, an individual must develop a personal relationship with reality. It's unhealthy to hold on to a belief contrary to experience. It causes a lot of anxiety and confusion. Beliefs are developed through experience or introjected from others. A child who is told there are crocodiles in the stream will believe it. They've no choice but to believe it. In Australia, there are crocodiles in the stream and this information will protect a child. If a child in Scotland is told there's a crocodile in the stream, then the child will stay away from the stream, reducing the chance of drowning, but will look a fool when they mention to their classmates the story of crocodiles in the Firth of Forth. The same child may believe they saw a crocodile in the Firth of Forth when they walked along the water's edge with their father and had it pointed out to them. The child saw the top of a car tire as it bobbed up and down in the water, but perceived it to be a crocodile. Human perception is set by their beliefs. If you have a bias for perceiving a certain thing then when there's ambiguity then you'll construct meaning based on the reality inside your beliefs regarding reality the difficulty arises when someone fishes the car tire out of the river, and we still insist we saw a crocodile. In human nature, the tendency to hold on to fiction as if it were reality and discount firm evidence is an epidemic of humans who are the most neurotic creatures of the animal kingdom. Imagine if the child was told if he didn't continue to believe the tire was a crocodile that his family and friends would abandon him. It would seem logical that the child could convince themselves that there is a crocodile in the river. Once they've strengthened their mind to hold on to the belief, they must create explanations to discredit contradictory evidence. The child explains that what has been retrieved from the river is indeed a tire. The crocodile has not been located and 'crocodile deniers' are using tyres to discredit the belief of a crocodile. The argument is made that 'crocodile deniers' are not looking for the crocodile properly. But how do you disprove the existence of something if it does not exist? Things that don't exist can't be examined. If I was to state 'I believe somewhere in the universe, there's a pair of underpants ruling over a planet of Betamax video recorders' it would be impossible for anyone to present an argument to disprove my belief. We have been to the moon, so we can provide evidence it's not made of cheese, but we have not visited every place in the universe, so, although it's ridiculous, we cannot disprove there's a race of Betamax video recorders being ruled over by a pair of Y front underpants. This is the reasoning people use when attempting to prove there's a God. 'You can't prove it doesn't exist, therefore it does.' Bonkers, absolutely bonkers, and yet people embrace it, defend it and will die for it. Most therapists come to the profession after experiencing some kind of therapy themselves and finding a series of insights have assisted them to become better adjusted, or at least to understand they're not as well adjusted as they previously thought. Counsellors and psychotherapists usually continue receiving therapy throughout their lives to facilitate growth and change. For many, the subject of counselling and psychotherapy has become like a religion. Many therapists may feel the experience of therapy has brought them closer to a spiritual power and feel their insights will assist others to find insights and experience transcendence. Counselling and psychotherapy have been developed over the past century to provide people with a venue to explore personal issues in what's designed to be 'a safe, judgement-free environment.' Although counselling has been developed scientifically from psychological research, it's the unfortunate human tendency to apply something supernatural to their experience. For many individuals who embark on therapy, the experience of counselling can be powerful with moments of insight and clarity. For many the experience is like a spiritual revelation, so it's not surprising many who practice counselling do so within the organisation of a church or other spiritual establishment. Religion and counselling do have one similarity, the promise of acceptance.

Humans are driven by a natural tendency to find meaning in all things. They do this by a process of pattern matching and correlation. They see patterns in the clouds and in tea leaves and give those patterns meaning. This tendency has helped us to learn and advance science and medicine. There's no doubt we can see a relationship between fire and heat, and as a result our species can create and control fire. We have been able to see the relationship between sickness and hygiene. The tendency to see patterns in things can cause erroneous conclusions. For example, people would blame unfortunate events upon people with little reason. Perhaps a new traveller to the village has coincided with crops failing to grow or the milk turning sour. The tendency of our ancestors was perhaps to exile or burn the poor unfortunate traveller for being a witch. Crying 'witch' at an unfortunate, vulnerable individual is not something confined to the ignorance of bygone times as it still goes on today in parts of India and Africa. We're shocked to find in our media reports that children from these countries are put through terrifying exorcisms by their ministers and sometimes killed because of our tendency to believe. Our inborn tendency to survive and thrive by seeing patterns also causes us to take part in ridiculous acts of abuse and inhumanity. There's also the apparently less serious belief that arises from erroneous correlations. Some will see patterns in tea leaves or see a certain number of magpies and as a result make a judgement regarding their future. Others will see occurrences as a symbolic answer to their prayers from the God of the universe. The pattern seen is directly related to the individual's own experiences or mind set. If a child likes 'Star Wars' then it's more likely he will see a picture in the clouds of an Ewok and a Christian might see a cloud in the shape of Mary, mother of Jesus. We all have a mindset determining what we're most likely to see, this is why inkblot tests are so interesting. Each person will see a different picture in the random pattern, and it's likely to reveal something unique to their own mind set and tendency to perceive certain things. The tendency to randomly attribute meaning goes further than clouds and tea leaves, but also dictates how we perceive everything in the world, and this will determine our reactions, attitudes and sense of safety. If we view anyone who is not a member of our religion as a sinner and deserving of death on the fiery day of Armageddon, then it's likely we'll also feel little genuine compassion for them - an extreme example of this is the Westboro Baptist Church who celebrates the death of anyone who does not conform to their extreme views. Our mindset is so easily moulded into baseless beliefs that most humans can be persuaded to commit horrible crimes. Adolph Hitler could convince a Nation some people are subhuman and there's virtue in bringing about their death. The example of Hitler's genocide appears extreme, but the God of the Abrahamic Bible also advocates and commands' sickening genocide, and no one bats an eyelid. *"The people of Samaria must bear the consequences of their guilt because they rebelled against their God. An invading army will kill them, their little ones dashed to death against the ground, their pregnant women ripped open by swords." (Hosea 13:16 NLT)*

It's through the study of seasonal cycles and the nature of animals we have been able to thrive as a species. Understanding the world gives us confidence we have some control over our own wellbeing. We may not always understand the world accurately. A child may look into a lake and see his reflection and assume it's an alternative reality. An adult with an understanding can teach the child about reflections, but in ancient Briton the children were told the reflection was exactly as it appeared, it was another world. Humans create meaning, humans crave meaning, and humans are meaning junkies. Without meaning or purpose, existence is futile. This kind of thinking can lead to disrepair and has existential philosophers fighting nihilism with nothing to fill the void of apparent meaninglessness. It's enough to drive you bonkers. If we look at the universe without preconceived beliefs, then it becomes purposeless and for many this is a terrifying prospect. This is not a pessimistic view, there's nothing pessimistic about a universe without purpose or meaning, it's our drive to find meaning leading us to disrepair. Our problem with finding meaning is we're looking for it outside ourselves, perhaps in a book on religion or philosophy, but finding true meaning could be like looking for something that's not there. We look for it because we're programmed to do so. If we find true, ultimate meaning, then great, we can relax; but you cannot prove there's 'no meaning' to the universe any more than you can prove there's 'no God,' or 'no unicorns.' How can you prove something does not exist until you have searched every solitary part of the universe? You can't. Those who search for the meaning of it all, are condemned never to find it. Finding meaning to the universe is futile. If the universe is just a simulation created by an operator to understand the process of universal physics and biological evolution, then the people generated by the simulation can't be satisfied by the answer. It would mean they were created just to satisfy their creator's curiosity. Is God the operator of this universe? Even the God of the Bible could be seen as a computer operator and the humans within it would be simulations. What would be the difference? God cannot be seen, and yet sees everything, but rarely gets involved. It appears the purpose of life for his creation is to fulfill their function to love and obey him. Rather like a vacuum cleaner, humans have a function. Ecclesiastes 12 verse 13 says: *After all this, there's only one thing to say: "Have reverence for God, and obey his commands, because this is all that we were created for."* A child playing a computer game requires the same of all his characters. The argument that computer generated characters can't be compared to real life is not applicable because there we have acknowledged to create computers beyond human abilities, self awareness is absent until the right kind of programming is invented. Humans are nothing more than an amalgamation of separate parts giving the illusion of oneness. Buddhists acknowledge the self is an illusion and made up of five aggregates of 'form, feeling consciousness, perception and mental formations,' and any experience of a real complete self is because of these aggregates working together to form an illusion, which benefits the organism who attempts to sustain itself. There's absolutely no reason to think there's an operator of this universe, but we know humans and all other life is a product of various elements. We're a compound believing it's a self. Some people may feel offended by such a viewpoint, but I have never heard a counter argument. Biologically we're an organism of chemical parts. The belief we have a self appears to give us something to protect, and as a result our consciousness avoids danger and attempts to elevate its social status and increase its sense of comfort. Oddly enough, we also protect anything we associate with our sense of self. We protect our children and we protect our community. We may even protect the image of a football team or political party, even though we're sometimes shamed by their actions. The sense of a self is a survival instinct, and by protecting our group, we also protect our genes and values. Genes and values are the two things we leave after we're dead . Our children carry our genes into an eternity of generations, and our perceptions and values are carried on in the same way through learning. The genes themselves don't need meaning, they need not understand anything, they're just self-replicating cells with the ability to exist forever without purpose or meaning. This makes it appear our 'sense of self' and consciousness is nothing but an effect of evolution. The question, 'what's the meaning or purpose of life?'-Presupposes that there's a meaning. This is difficult to grasp because of the innate tendency to see meaning in everything, including the most silly of cloud shapes, tea leaves, and ink blotches. To consider existence is meaningless flies in the face of our programming which drives us to cherish community, family, children and self. And yet, experience tells us they're temporary and have meaning for us personally. How do we live in the knowledge we're conscious and alive and yet impermanent? People not only cling to meaning, but also to immortality. The evidence suggests that even down to the fundamental physics of the 3rd law of thermodynamics, the universe itself is temporary. People are left with metaphysical arguments regarding immortality, and when people put their faith in something they've never experienced, then the argument becomes a juvenile philosophical discussion regarding fantasy. There's no argument countering a belief in the impermanent or the metaphysical.

Mankind blindly seeks meaning and purpose based on the ideas of charismatic leaders who've exploited followers for millennia. Through religion you can guide people to commit the most horrible of crimes. The pay-off for followers is a sense of purpose and freedom from the anxiety of oblivion. Understanding spiritual beliefs based on nothing more than fantasy cause people to do the most stupid things helps us realise how dangerous the hunger for meaning and immortality can be. To do stupid things requires special thinking. We always feel happier if we feel secure. The thinking which is dangerous is the kind making us feel secure knowing that martyrdom is a positive action. Homosexuality or following another religion is worthy of death in the Christian Bible. To feel secure in such an outlook on reality cannot help but alienate you from the sections of mankind who do not adopt your belief system. To believe people are worthy of death in the great day of Armageddon is to be more than a little judgemental. Can you hold such beliefs and still be a credible talking therapist? Counsellors have to deal with their own sense of meaninglessness, and could come under the influence of baseless religious ideas. How can a counsellor accept an individual unconditionally if they believe they're worthy of death? More so, how can they truly experience empathy with a client who's outgrown the confines of religion and is coming to terms with the reality of living in a universe that has no purpose or meaning? Within an infinite void of meaninglessness, the mathematical probability of life becomes an inevitability. Fuelled by infinite possibilities, the actualisation process can create life through natural selection. The rock had no meaning until the ape used it to crack open a nut, or the man used it to build his house. The stream had no meaning until the tree absorbed its goodness and until the fish laid their eggs. The South Pole had no meaning until it became the goal of the explorer to reach it, and oil and coal had no purpose until man found it useful for fuel. The consequences of an infinite universe are within the void of infinity something beautiful will happen. It will happen without purpose or meaning, but we may find it meaningful, we may find purpose for it. We're a working part of the universe; we are life. We may exist without ultimate meaning, but our relationship to the universe is special. The universe itself is unconscious and unaware of itself. There is no illusion of self or ego to bruise. The universe has no mind and is like a sleeping unborn who has no awareness. And yet we're awake, we're conscious and self aware. We are the universes becoming conscious of itself in a small way. In the words of Carl Sagan. "We are a way for the Cosmos to know itself." If each individual was to embrace the fact they don't know and can't know the universe with which they're a part, then everyone would be a scientist. Every person on the planet, every animal, fish and every piece of vegetation is part of the one universe. It's something we're all a part of and yet something we can never come to know fully in our lifetime. With every discovery scientists make, the universe becomes more aware of itself through us. But what has religion or theism offered that has opened the minds of individuals. When it comes to truth, science eats away at the falsehoods of religion with every new discovery. I personally cannot think of one religiously inspired idea that has replaced a scientific fact. People don't respect truth, they would much rather have a quick fix of well meaning myth, and when this does not fit reality they become neurotic. Actualisation in the universal sense requires patience. It does not presuppose meaning, it merely means something wonderful will happen for no other reason than mathematical probability. If we decide God created the universe and all life in it, then we take away the beauty of the natural tendency for the universe to grow with nothing to guide it but the potential coming from its scale and resources. Meaninglessness, but with the ingredient of infinite potential. No divine guidance required. Our innate tendency to find meaning is our basis for creating a God. Carl Jung was acquainted with the realities of instinctive programming that drives us to find meaning. He could identify the innate templates that give us the predisposition to perceive Gods, devils and angels when trying to make sense of the world. A blueprint of reality exists in our instincts, in what Jung called archetypes. Archetypes are all of our inborn instincts which act as an initial instruction booklet which also provides an initial perceptual mindset. Each archetype is like a computer program with its own folder where specific information is recorded and stored. Folders for recognising a mother and a father figure and gathering enough information to interact with reality. The fact we have instincts means we've a predisposition to perceive the world from a point of view that will fulfil our programmed needs as they change from moment to moment. The need for quiet, sex, food, water, acknowledgement and socialisation will all contribute to how we find meaning in life. We may attempt to sanitise our taboo instincts by altering their meaning. The need for sex is sanitised as romance and love when it's in fact our instinctive drive to procreate. However, you want to present your instincts and drive. It's important not to lose a sense of honesty around our intentions and needs. Many people hide behind a façade of virtue and compassion. Perhaps they become ministers or follow a career in social care to reinforce this self concept. Most times the individual is caring and empathic, but some who follow such a path are bullies, abusers or have a pathological desire to control others. Many people hide behind a façade because the truth regarding their motives and the meaning behind their actions are distorted in their own mind, so they achieve their goal of domination while maintaining a sense of esteem. Whatever the motivation behind a person's actions, it's how we apply meaning to the situation that dictates the perception. Self-concept is important to humans. An individual who commits crimes against fellow humans will rarely take responsibility for their actions because this would mean their self concept would need to change. The fear of losing self esteem and the respect (including the control) of others is too much to bear for many narcissistic types. Jean-Paul Sartre used the term 'Bad faith' to describe self deception. Many people will live according to the direction and dictates of family and culture, rather according to one's own organismic promptings. Some people may have the desire to become a doctor or start a business as an electrician, but because of the misogynistic values of the family or culture, the woman allows herself to pursue goals of being a mother and homemaker. She sees her future and plans her goals based on the ideals of other people rather than authentically, she has in effect become a puppet, being controlled, manipulated and by internalising those external values to create an unsatisfactory existence. The belief in a 'God' makes the situation more difficult, a belief that comes with eternal punishment and unworthiness of love and acceptance into a community. To form a self-concept which deviates from 'God's' requirements can render an individual a sense of low self worth. Alienation from 'God' means you have no purpose, worthy to be burned as the chaff. Meanings are unique to each individual, but humans desire to be consistent with their social group. When we've like-minded others around us, we can take comfort in our own beliefs, meanings and purposes. We may adjust our understanding of the world to conform to the understandings of our family, peers or co-workers.

Religion provides something humans crave more than food and water. This 'something' is the provision of acceptance. Acceptance is something we crave from our parents and our social group. It gives the feeling of safety and security. There's the certainty of survival in a social group. As much as I try to think of an example, I find it impossible to think of a successful individual who's not been part of a network of humans, either socially, as part of a family or as part of a business group. Acceptance has a direct effect upon our ability to be happy. Abraham Maslow knew this when he included 'Love and Belonging' at the third level of the hierarchy of needs as it gives the information we need to test our own worth in the world and develop a positive self concept with the feeling of security or low self esteem. Maslow was right to place the need for love and belonging at the third stage of his hierarchy, because it's at this stage we can transcend this need and have our esteem needs fulfilled; however, the need for love and belonging goes even deeper into our needs, as even as an infant we need the acceptance of our Mother to be cared for and have our basic needs of food and safety fulfilled, it's a fact that any child who is rejected by its mother will probably develop at a slower rate or even die. This is the importance of acceptance and when we don't receive it, it's not surprising many humans will experience despair and panic. This is manifested as anxiety disorders and depression. Love and acceptance is a provision bringing the promise of life to those who are cared for in a community. If you're part of a religion, then you may feel even in times of isolation you're still loved and cared for by an almighty God. I remember when I was a child, I would argue with my friends about who had the best dad. The argument had nothing to do with their good qualities, but how one dad could beat the other one in a fight. My dad was a part-time soldier, so I would always win the argument by telling my friends my dad would blow their dad up with a missile. A demonstration of his awesome power was never needed, all that mattered was we felt secure and safe with our strong fathers who loved us. People's perception of God is similar. People believe their God is powerful and could defeat the enemy and can give them a portion of this strength when requested through prayer. Most Gods, even the peaceful Jesus, make the promise they'll one day bring genocide to groups of people who do not worship them. To be loved by such a figure is surely an absolute protection. Not all love is unconditional. The love of a father has rules attached to it. Perhaps a father will insist you're polite and kind, that you eat all your food, that you do your homework, and that you brush your teeth. These rules are basic and easy to follow and even if they're deviated from, the loving father will encourage the child to understand the value of such behaviour. Some fathers may go a little over the top and hate the child who does not fulfill their expectations. A father who hates his child to the point that they'll not speak to them or acknowledge their existence will be classed as neglectful and overly critical of their child. The father we see in Gods is like a critical father in the sense he requires complete devotion and promises to either kill people who deviate or at least to condemn them to an eternity of torture. This kind of love is critical and controlled by the use of threats. The child able to obey will feel secure, but what about the child who cannot obey? Humans are full of people in religion who've difficulty obeying the rules of their religion and fall short of the love of their God and also as a result fall short of the love of their own families if they're allowed to find out. Some people feel extreme guilt for breaking the rules of their religion by breaking rules on what 'should' be believed, said and thought. Many people fall in love with someone who is of another culture, belief system or in a way that offends their religious sexual laws. This anxiety is powerful, life controlling and most of all brainwashed into us from birth with love and life dangled as a carrot to the obedient ass. When a baby is born it has no beliefs or expectations of this world. Everything is new and brings a sense of wonder. The child will use its mouth and hands to investigate the world, and as it does, it grows in both knowledge and skills. Every new piece of knowledge the child acquires is stored as a hypothesis and a guidebook of the world. A hypothesis is a belief open to change through experience. Babies are the epitome of an open mind as they'll constantly update how they perceive the world. Hypothetical thinking is the true door to knowledge because it prevents absolutism. The opposite of Hypothetical thinking is dogmatic thinking. Dogmatic thinking will not change in the face of new information. Dogmatic thinking gives people a feeling of security because it offers an individual the sense of prediction in the world. It comes with strong biases which colour perception, and as a result any faults in perception are not noticed or even dismissed as nonsense. This dogmatic thinking causes racism, sexism, and all kinds of prejudice. It's impossible to be a counsellor if you hold on to dogmatic thinking as this view will mean you're accepting the client if they fulfil your criteria for acceptance. A counsellor who believes abortion is murder is faced with a dilema when presented with a pregnant 13-year-old girl who is considering an abortion. Any attempt to accept the client would definitely cause some anxiety to the counsellor. You cannot be a counsellor with such a dogmatic attitude. Hypothetical thinking gives the counsellor a humble view of their own beliefs and as a result they'll not experience anxiety when those beliefs are challenged. It's simple, hypothetical thinking is open minded and ready to test beliefs against reality, and change them to match the experience. As already stated, the baby has no beliefs and is ready to explore the world and learn. The child will develop attachments to its mother and father, perhaps to its siblings and extended family, and this brings a sense of security. It's natural to feel emotional about those attachments, especially when they're severed. The pathology of human experience comes into play when people we're close to threaten to abandon us because we don't share their dogmatic beliefs. For a child, believing in Santa is fun, and it's fun for the parent too; but sometimes a child might no longer believe in Santa but still professes this belief to maintain a positive relationship with their parents. The need for love and attachment to parents, family or a group is strong and linked to our survival. If his clan abandoned the hunter gatherer, then he would starve to death. So family and attachments are a powerful incentive for survival and we'll probably adjust our behaviour and thinking to maintain such attachments and remain loved and accepted. At some point the conservative impulse comes into play, which gives humans a tendency to become more rigid in our thinking, so we can feel secure. We see the conservative impulse in people who've had difficulty accepting change. It causes the experience of grief to become long term and complicated as we cannot adjust to the loss of a loved one. It can be something as simple as becoming annoyed because someone says happy holiday instead of happy Christmas or people of different races moving into your street. The conservative impulse causes much anxiety and anger for people because it suppresses contemptuous of change. The tendency to think hypothetically disappears in most people as they grow older, as they rely on the programming of their younger years to guide their future, but in a world of constant change, this cannot result in happiness.

A RANT ON ETHICS, SIN AND INTROJECTION.

How do we know what's good? Everyone conforms to society's rules and makes up their own mind. Scientifically, there's no objective way of identifying good, however scientists agree to work ethically based on respect toward human participants in research. Some people claim to have the Bible or other holy book as their moral guide, and others claim to be guided by a philosophy. The threat of hell or eternal death and the promise of eternal life encourages many to conform to certain rules and thinking. The argument is made by some theists "If you don't believe in God, where do you get your moral guidance from?" From a Christian point of view humans are faulty, with a tendency to do bad. The cure for the disease of sin is redemption by obeying the words of a man who was sacrificed to appease God's anger. Christian religions believe humans are inherently sinful and if it was left to humans, the world would become a violent, lust driven place of depravity. The examples of Sodom and Gomorrah, the world before Noah's flood and the Biblical reports of Pagan practices in Canaan and the shocking practices of Israelites who turned away from God are examples of what humans will degenerate to if left to decide for themselves what's 'good and bad'. Good and bad are relative. If we accept a book like the Bible as a moral guide then we're vulnerable to endorsing the pink and fluffy verses with the unpalatable 'God commissioned acts,' of mass genocide and ethnic cleansing, sex slavery of women and children, murder of children of a different religion by bashing them against rocks, the use of incest to continue the family line, stoning victims of rape and protecting sex offenders, endorsement of child abuse, and also offering your daughters for men to rape to protect visiting angels. Good and bad are relative, even Christians choose the parts of the bible they find palatable and forget to attribute the horrible 'God commissioned acts' to his personality. It appears even they're deciding for themselves what's right and wrong. Anything can be justified by using handpicked scriptures. This is how the Catholic Church could inspire people to take part in the genocide of the crusades as well as torture and execute heretics. Even in today's world we find religions justifying the excommunication of children to where their own families reduce contact with them in their own home, where infants have their genitals mutilated and scarred from the rest of their lives in a religiously inspired ritual of circumcision. Religion takes away peoples natural/ inborn tendency toward an empathic morality and allows themselves to act like psychopaths who allow the genital mutilation of a child.

A counsellor who believes in a creator is not a problem as long as the values of a religion do not involve adopting a psychopathic viewpoint and the condemnation of people who reject your faith's values. Believing in a God does not disqualify a person from being a counsellor as long as it's a hypothetical belief. We can sometimes believe something is true until evidence to the contrary. Believing there's a fish in an empty pond won't kill you unless you tell people of your village that God says you can only eat food the pond provides, then your people will have a good chance of starvation. The problem arises when belief becomes dogmatic, closed to adaptation to facts. change. Beliefs about the creator's personality, his morality, requirements and promises for the future are delusions if they're without evidence. Many Christians and Muslims point to their holy books as evidence in a circle of reasoning that could stretch even the patience of Job. The circular reasoning is presented as "I know it's the truth because it's in the Bible, and I know the Bible contains facts because God says it does in the Bible." This reasoning is an existential paradox that fills the believer with confidence, but if you follow this kind of reasoning as a counsellor, it might be worth considering a few more years of training and therapeutic support for yourself. How can someone who is deluded be an effective guide to those suffering? Counsellors must have a clear view in their minds of what's true, fallacy and knowability and respect the process that identifies each. it's the counsellor's job to assist clients to identify misleading perceptions and come to a more logical view of reality based on evidence. Reality, based on evidence, has a strong base for growth and maturity. The unwillingness to have such a hypothetical and scientific approach to reality disqualifies you as a counsellor. If you believe you experienced divine inspiration and literally experience God, but can't prove it wasn't a psychotic episode brought on by mental illness or an experience of euphoria during hypnotic like prayer, then you're dishonest with yourself and others and as a result have disqualified yourself from being a counsellor. A counsellor must be congruent or genuine. To delude yourself and expect to have the maturity to help people who are looking to address imbalances in their lives is ridiculous. As Jesus says *"If the blind lead the blind, will they not both fall in the pit." (Matthew 15:4)* If a counsellor believes it's acceptable to absorb values and beliefs into their moral reality without examination, then it's difficult to see how they could assist someone to strive towards autonomy. A counsellor who dogmatically has faith in anything in the face of contrary evidence, has suspended critical thinking and accepted something into their reality, can't help but affect their approach to counselling. To believe something so important and fundamental to reality is dangerous, especially if they declare loyalty to that God. Believing that there's a creator means we're likely to attribute qualities to God that will be based on introjection or personal bias. Whichever it is, it will probably be a dogmatic viewpoint. Most people's dogmatic viewpoint is that God, the Universe or the Spirit's unquestionably good. Any suggestion this is not true is met with resistance, even if it's only a light discussion. If such a conversation were to occur in the counselling room, then the counsellor may find their frame of reference returned to their own threatened faith as they're compelled to defend a cherished creator.

COLD READING: ON BECOMING THE PROJECTED ARCHETYPE.

Psychotherapists and counsellors have the power of cult leaders and possess the secret knowledge of a prophet or shaman; or at least this is how many clients view them and they'll follow their therapist like a disciple following a guru. This sounds incredible, but it's the experienced therapist who understands how dangerous this power can be and how easy it can be to fall into the trap of becoming a spiritual guide rather than a talking therapist. If you check out some of the pages on Facebook you'll find many counsellors, life coaches and psychotherapists who offer spiritual guidance and insight based on their own spiritual beliefs. Some advocate a belief in angels, God, Reiki and spirits for healing. Cold reading is a clever way to convince an individual that you have supernatural abilities or secret occult knowledge. I don't mean to upset people who claim to have special spiritual abilities; but the fact is, whether they accept it or not (because some believe they've special abilities) cold reading is a technique employed by the most successful fortune tellers, psychics, mediums, cult leaders and other practitioners who claim to have spiritual gifts. For most people who receive a personal reading from these 'spiritual practitioners', it can result in the client having faith and trust in the practitioner which is developed without much skill at all; for many all that's needed is the gift of the gab combined with pregnant pauses. The rapport that's created by such practitioners is truly awe inspiring, even beautiful, and it can also be terrifying to watch. You can see individuals who've experienced bereavement being misled into (or sucked into) the belief that they're receiving a message from beyond the grave. The strength of rapport that a cold reader develops with a client is something that can take an inexperienced psychotherapist or counsellor months to fully establish. It's frustrating to know that by pretending to have psychic powers that the rightly disposed client will give you their complete unconditional trust. The client is likely to accept the counsellor because it's built into the instincts of every human to identify an individual who appears to have secret esoteric knowledge. Gurus, witch doctors, Shamen, wise women, elders and clergy are viewed as sources of secret wisdom that will enhance our lives. C.G. Jung discussed these phenomena when identifying archetypes. Archetypes exist within the human psyche and assist us to identify people who'll perform certain roles. An archetype is rather like an empty jelly mould that certain people can fill. In their purest form they'll manifest in dreams as spiritual figures, angels or devils; but they all represent a mundane function. A motherly figure can fill the mother archetype as she has qualities of nurturing and unconditional love or at least this should be the case. If the mother in reality fills the archetype with neglect, harm and love with conditions then this will leave the child with a damaged view of reality and low self esteem. This does not affect whether the mother is accepted, she will be accepted by the child because she is the resource for filling the desires of the archetype and without a mother we will not last long. The Shamanic Archetype developed as a way of identifying the skilled person in the village. It was the wise Homoerectus (early man) who taught his village to create sharp cutting tools from stone. He would've also taught his students to create and control fire. Technical knowledge of fire and the creation of tools was magical knowledge to early man. Even the masters of mathematics who created the ancient buildings in Babylon and Egypt were viewed as having secret knowledge, a fact we see preserved in the principles of Freemasonry which is saturated in secret symbols and archetypal imagery. So the wisdom of the archetypal shaman in the clothes of a counsellor or the cold reader is accepted unconditionally by many persons who seek wisdom and guidance. Developing rapport is key to successful cold reading because rapport is based on trust and in some cases blind faith. Sometimes new therapists who are new to the counselling process report difficulty establishing rapport from the important early stages of the therapeutic relationship. It can be frustrating for counselling students but as they develop their empathic skills, the ability to create rapport is enhanced and becomes easy to use as an intentional therapeutic tool. I believe that the experienced cold reader has learned to do a lot more than use the skills already mentioned. Cold readers through experience have fine tuned their skills of intuition. When I say intuition, I mean that they're able to watch body language and tone of voice and dress to gain ideas about the client's well being and other aspects of life. Just by assessing someone's age a cold reader can assume how many people are in that individual's life and how many people they've lost. If an individual is in their seventies, then it's likely that they've suffered multiple losses and also have children and grandchildren. They may have retired and miss the role that a job supplies. Effective cold readers will have empathic skills and be quick to get an idea of a client's emotions and build rapport based on their understanding of those emotions. Using rapport as a therapeutic tool is a foundational principle of Neuro Linguistic Programming. Psychologists have observed that when people have a good rapport, it can be observed that their stance, posture and gestures mirror each other. The speed, tone and volume of speech is the same. The more mirroring and matching there is then the greater the rapport and the stronger the trust is between two individuals. Usually mirroring and matching will happen unconsciously when two people 'click'. This can be observed in everyday life between businessmen who are working together on a project that will make them both rich and between friends who are 'catching up'. You'll especially see the beauty of rapport between people who are flirting in a reciprocal dance of courtship. Mirroring and matching indicates that the people in the conversation are focused on each other and become one organism. This happens unconsciously as they match each other's communication pattern to maintain rapport. You can watch people who are in deep rapport, dancing as they stand and talk while mirroring and matching. you can see them, in order to maintain a comfortable communicative proximity, constantly moving in a circle that can take perhaps only three minutes to make one revolution. It can be a humorous dance to watch but it's also beautiful as it's a unique human characteristic. It takes great skill and grace to develop and maintain rapport artificially, to manipulate certain variables, with the purpose of influencing the client's unconscious so they feel a deep connection to you. To accomplish this, it's important to mirror and match voice and physical communication with a client in order to develop rapport quickly. This saves time and money for the client and increases the sense of satisfaction they obtain from therapy. Gaining rapport fulfils the client's natural need to be accepted, loved and acknowledged. It can't be emphasised enough how important it is to develop this quality at the beginning of the therapeutic relationship as first impressions are extremely powerful and make a lasting impression on the client. Counsellors and psychotherapists like to emphasise the 'individual,' and this is reflected in much of the pop psychology literature, which describes how to change your life for the better. As the therapist gains experience they realise that although we've unique experiences, we tend to have a finite amount of emotional reactions that can be generated within these unique experiences. The result of such a realisation is that we're all pretty much the same; the fact that people believe they're personally as unique as their experiences adds to the 'illusion of wisdom' that a cold reader or experienced therapist appears to possess. Many experienced therapists realise all humans are built the same way and that we experience the same physical sensations, emotions and reactions with variances in our perception of these experiences. This is used to the advantage of the experienced psychotherapist because they're able to express generalities, which increase rapport between client and counsellor because these generalities appear to portray a deep understanding from the client's point of view. For example, you can gain quick rapport with a client when they express that they're stressed or depressed when you ask the insightful gem of a question, such as:

"Also, is your sleep pattern affected? You find that your thoughts become overly active when you're in bed?"

This insightful expression of a generality appears psychic to a client and some will even believe that the therapist has psychic powers but these symptoms are experienced by every stress induced insomniac on the planet. Most therapists understand that the client perceives in the practitioner something that's needed, a guide or someone who can tell us the comforting truth of reality. Transference will also be a factor. If we feel a client experiences an instant 'like' to the therapist it's probably because they experienced a nurturing individual in the past that the therapist reminds them of in some way. Usually transference is a negative feeling and happens when the memories of a significant adult are evoked. As a result we might meet someone who reminds us unconsciously of an arrogant and angry school teacher and as a result immediately feel an irrational fear. Transference can also be the result of an unfulfilled pattern. For example the need for a mother is important for a child's survival and the 'mother archetype' (Innate Template) requires that certain nurturing characteristics be craved for and sought. These unfulfilled characteristics can become projected onto a certain candidate who fits the criteria, such as an aunt or grandmother if the natural mother is not available. The experience of a maternal figure is not necessary for the pure archetype(Innate template)to be a source of transference. The natural tendency for attachment to the maternal figure is as strong as the need for food. As mothers are revered by their children, the maternal figure becomes a 'goddess like' figure which fulfils the individual's archetypal needs. In this way the replacement maternal figure has become a blank movie screen to which the mother archetype has been projected. As children get older, their innate templates are altered by 'experience' of the maternal figure and projections onto future maternal figures such as a mate will be affected by these experiences, however, the Shaman archetype for many people is rarely fulfilled. Much of the apparent wisdom and secret knowledge that humans instinctively need is fulfilled by the 'insightful gems' of an archetype figure. In this way, the client projects onto the therapist their instinctive shamanistic archetype which is the reason that the Counsellor/Psychotherapist, Priest, Tarot Reader and psychic are all accepted by clients as having secret knowledge and become effectively 'the Projected Archetype'. The problem with some less mature therapists is that they experience counter-transference and accept the role of 'Projected Archetype,' and thus risk counter-transference, effectively becoming a spiritual guide. It's sad to see this happen, as this type of counter-transference represents the need of the therapists to have their ego tickled, and weakens the client's ability to remain independent of therapy.

The power of cold reading was brought to my attention while I was still studying Counselling at TyneMet College. I was aware of the automatic trust clients placed in me as a Counsellor with an assumption of benevolence and absolute trust. Before I used any skills or even introduced myself; clients appeared to feel accepted by me in the Rogerian 'unconditional way'. I was seen as a professional who was experienced, without me needing to prove myself in any way. This was used to therapeutic advantage, but I was somewhat confused at how easy it was to become a trusted professional without needing to prove myself what so ever. I was fascinated to find that outside the therapy arena that one thing could take this trust to a far greater level, to a charismatic 'cult leader' effect. This was the day I decided to help out a charity by doing tarot cards at their summer fair. I believed that because it was a simple summer fair that the public would view my tarot stall in a light hearted way, but I couldn't have been more wrong, dangerously wrong. As a counsellor I was viewed as a benevolent professional with special training, but as a tarot reader I was viewed as much more. I got the sense with some individuals that care should be taken to protect them as they began to spill every bottled up emotion of their long life within the space of a ten minute reading. This was even more fascinating as we weren't in a private consulting room but rather sitting at an open stall in a public fair. This, I agree, sounds dangerous, and in the wrong hands it has proven to be on many occasions. It reminds me of the power of many cult leaders who are accepted unconditionally by their followers. The followers of cult leaders have faith in their master and we hear many strange stories of intelligent, wealthy people donating their life savings and their homes to their adored messiah. During the 20th century there were various doomsday cults that required men to donate their families and their wives to their messiah for his sexual gratification and later commit ritualistic suicide. They do this with complete faith that they'll receive a spiritual reward in the afterlife. You'll be glad to hear that none of this happened at the summer fair. I just found it fascinating to find that I could be so completely trusted for no other reason that I owned a packet of tarot cards. I was just a little unsettled as I realised how vulnerable people are in the presence of a blind and self serving guide. It could be argued that people who are followers of 'projected archetypes' such as tarot readers, psychics and cult leaders have a specific set of needs or neurosis which makes them susceptible to blindly following a deluded messiah, and I would agree with that idea. One of the needs these believers have unfulfilled is the need for acceptance and love. The need for love is in us all. With love comes companionship, family and security. Without love we would die as an infant which is why we need to identify people who fit maternal archetypes. Love is a life or death resource, and we'll alter our behaviour in order to receive it. Those who are starved of love will not distinguish between 'conditional' love and 'unconditional' love, and for them it's the starvation of love that entraps them. If acceptance and the Maslonian need for belonging are offered to the 'love starved' individual, it's swallowed like stagnant sewage water on drought stricken land. It quenches the thirst and gives temporary relief but it's also toxic and results in death. All spirituality is like this because it requires the individual to suspend critical thinking and adopt an altered perception of what they experience in order to continue to obtain love and acceptance. This poisonous water of conditional love is supplied by churches, God of the Bible, and other followers who thirst for acknowledgement from their Shamanistic archetypes. They experience a euphoric high as they bathe in the baseless belief that they're on the right path; in the same way an opium addict finds bliss in the chemical that destroys their life. I have been concerned that some counsellors have also taken a messianic cult leader attitude by writing advertisements and blogs that advocate their own spiritual beliefs in the power angels to guide clients. Other fallen counsellors make some shockingly ambiguous statements by suggesting that their talents may be enhanced by their own spiritual power. Many clients have been affected by counsellors who offer such baseless claims. The false hope is damaging because it requires faith and dependence on the counsellor who claims to have esoteric insight. Of course counsellors in some cases may genuinely believe they have special powers, but this just makes them more dangerous to vulnerable clients, after all, how can a deluded person help someone to assimilate reality and find balance? Yet it's the 'deluded blind guide' that attracts the most vulnerable to the contaminated waters of delusion. Cold reading is the ability to make convincing predictions or speculations about an individual's life, feelings and perspectives without ever meeting them before. It's practised by fortune tellers and mediums with notable success. People who've employed their services recommend them with enthusiasm and are convinced that the cold reader has special powers. This ability appears fascinating to the uneducated individual who has a 'desire to believe,' but the skills are based on nothing more than educated guesses and universal truths regarding human nature and the desire of the client to find meaning in what's said. Cold readers are not always aware that they're employing these skills. For many it's developed after many years of practice by employing techniques that work and dropping techniques that don't. To the educated psychologist it's obvious that the cold reader is misleading people, but when the client confirms that the information the cold reader has delivered has meaning for them, then the client and the reader gain stronger faith in the illusionary powers. Cold readers become increasingly convinced that they've psychic powers because of their positive results. It sounds ridiculous, but it's a social paradox of delusion played out in tragic circumstances. In effect, by validating another's belief, the cold reader's deluded beliefs regarding their own powers also become validated. Of course, for mutual validation to occur, there must be an emotional desire from the client to see into the future or to speak to the dead. Fulfilling the need gives the client hope and reassurance that there's something beyond this life. Cold readers also have hope and reassurance that there's more to life but more to the point they also get their ego tickled. The cold reader becomes validated in the sense that they're admired by people for having secret knowledge regarding the spirit world. The client and the sincere cold reader who believe that they've these powers have what on the surface appears to be a symbiotic relationship and feed off each other. It's beautiful, but there's no real benefit to the client as they're prevented from successfully completing a natural grief process. After all, how can you grieve for the loss of a loved one if they're still in communication with you from beyond the grave? Many people become obsessed with such cold readings to avoid the change that has already happened and as a result some people never marry again and spend their time still obeying dead parent's wishes out of respect and fear. The cold reader benefits from the addictive qualities of this relationship whether the client benefits or not. The cold reader is validated, praised and is paid for what they do. So calling this a symbiotic relationship would be wrong.

Unintentionally, the sincere cold reader is nothing more than a parasite which slowly feeds on their client's vulnerability. A parasite of course does not intentionally harm its host, but as it's true for a tapeworm, it's also true for the cold reader: if they didn't benefit in some way from the process of feeding from their host then they wouldn't bother doing it. The counsellor/psychotherapist needs to keep this in mind before employing any of the techniques that are used by such individuals. We do not want to just engage in therapy in order to validate ourselves at the expense of a client. We must always make sure that our relationship with the client is authentic, which means that we must be honest and aware of any tendency to be non genuine. Accepting a validating statement from a client may be well meant but if we swallow the validation like a thirsty fat dog on a hot day without examining it first, then we're allowing the client to feed our hungry ego. We need to be able to discern between genuine compliments and flattery, and certainly not allow a client to inflate our own ego. The principles of cold reading can be employed to help reinforce the client's trust in you as an experienced therapist and also conveys the message that you have a deep understanding of human nature. This is demonstrated by the aforementioned 'insightful gems.' Positive prejudice combined with evidence of your understanding regarding human experience is important for gaining unconditional trust. After you have acquired the trust and rapport with the client most of the work during the rest of the course of the therapeutic relationship will be much easier and will also achieve a lot more in a shorter time. This will give you a greater sense of worth as a therapist and save your client time and money. Counselling and psychotherapy are secular approaches to well-being. It's a peculiar statement, but not everyone agrees with this perspective and makes claims that there's a connection between faith and spirituality. Some even point to the works of C.G Jung to give credibility to their beliefs, joining the bandwagon of 'occultist hippies' who never understood what Jung was saying anyway. Therapists go through years of training to learn scientifically researched techniques that help an individual to explore their reality and discuss personal feelings and meanings that may have been hidden from awareness before receiving therapy. During therapy a client may feel that they've experienced spiritual enlightenment where they gain a more understandable perception of reality. Many clients and trainee counsellors confuse this life changing experience with some kind of spiritual power or deep shamanistic wisdom of the counsellor or psychotherapist. The therapist can be attributed as possessing esoteric knowledge which has been applied to the sessions. Many clients or trainee therapists suspect that the counsellor or psychotherapist has all the answers about the great questions of life including the question, what happens after death? And is there a god? Some clients embark on this by going to college to study psychotherapy in order to obtain this knowledge to find that the answers are nonexistent. The reality is that effective therapists have no answers to offer about such subjects. The client feels the euphoric change in their life because the counsellor has assisted them to harness their own inner wisdom which results in an altered state of consciousness in relation to their life. The difference between a counsellor and a cold reader is that the counsellor fosters autonomy and the inner wisdom of the client, whereas the cold reader fosters dependence in the client so they can retain power, an income and an ego boost. It could be that until the client embarked on counselling that the client's inner wisdom was inhibited due to the non acceptance of feelings such as hate or anger, which may be against personal values. Accepting these feelings for them would imply that they were in some way immoral or in possession of a bad character. Most people want a good reputation. Our values contribute to the image of who we aspire to be, but our feelings are who we are in reality. In many cultures feelings of hatred and resentment are classed as feelings of an immoral character. In other words, to experience a bad feeling toward another person implies that you have a serious character flaw, and it's natural when we become aware of such 'terrible' feelings that we'd reject and dislike ourselves if. If a man is constantly bullied by his boss to the point that he dreads coming into work then he would probably feel some negative emotions regarding this situation. If his values prevent him from acknowledging that he feels angry or even hates his boss then he cannot gain an accurate perspective to deal with the issue. There's so many reasons that an individual may not acknowledge feelings, most of the time it's because they're convinced that these feelings are bad and do not want to believe they could experience feelings such as envy or hatred. Seeing the whole situation clearly means that we must be aware of our own feelings as part of that situation, it's then that we can deal with the situation effectively. This is why an individual who comes for counselling experiences euphoria as they see the world in a different way. The feeling of joy happens because the client begins to allow their personal perspective to come into awareness and complete the picture, and with this comes a new sense of self acceptance. To accept and even love parts of yourself that you have denied from awareness is a powerful experience which many would confuse with a spiritual enlightenment. Annoyingly, we find that cold readers appear to be able to achieve a 'sense' of enlightenment within a much shorter time frame than a counsellor, although this may be an illusionary experience. This is annoying, because a cold reader disempowers the client, leading them to believe that their service is the avenue to acquire secret knowledge for life. Cold readers evoke the shaman archetype and clients are all too willing to accept the cold readers' wild guesses and ideas from 'Pagan Weekly' as representing factual truths about the universe. This is dangerous because dependence upon the cold reader means the client will be under their control rather than being led by their own reasoning and actualising tendency. This is how cult leaders attract followers to do whatever is asked, and yet if the techniques could be applied therapeutically by a counselling therapist then this would be a powerful tool that could be applied as a means of quickening the client's willingness to take part in open dialogue. The environment that the therapist creates for the client is safe in the sense that they're free of judgement and condemnation. The client can be criticised and belittled by their own thoughts within the therapeutic setting. It may take several sessions before a client truly feels safe enough to become open and express their feelings. The client has limited financial resources, so it's useful to the client to be helped to feel the connection with the counsellor as quickly as possible as this will save them time and money. However this is not always as easy as we'd like it to be. Even getting a client to accept that they feel deep hatred or resentment toward a family member who's stolen their mother's life savings can take a full session. Even when they express their negative feelings, they may find that they struggle between experiences of conflicting values. Conflicting values and feelings are painful and contribute to the slowness of therapeutic change. For example the true feelings of anger and hatred may be kept from full awareness by minimising the experience which alters the perception. This could be expressed as "My boss and I don't always see eye to eye," instead of, "I feel anger toward my boss and feel that I could happily decapitate him with a spoon." Frustration regarding the amount of time counselling and psychotherapy take is something that a client won't express directly but I always get the message when they express the desire to visit a fortune teller or medium to gain answers to their dilemmas or problems. It frustrates me even more when they report that the fortune teller was able to understand the way they feel without ever meeting them beforehand. The ability to make someone feel that you know what's going on in their life without receiving much information creates fascination, trust and faith which may be misplaced, but is the envy of counselling therapists because we have to work to gain rapport with a client without misleading them that we've special powers. However I believe that it's possible to identify exactly what the fortune teller is doing that makes their predictions so accurate and what it's about those predictions that evoke unconditional trust. With this knowledge the counselling therapist could help the client to conclude their therapy in a much shorter time with potentially more satisfying results. It's important, of course, not to mislead clients into believing that we have special powers or spiritual abilities where there's no evidence to support such claims. I am assuming that all fortune tellers and psychics are employing the principles of cold reading and don't have these occult abilities either. Cold readers use ingredients which are employed to facilitate the client to feel rapid trust resulting in the client feeling safe enough to open up at a rate of speed that a therapist would give their right arm to achieve. This is something that the most experienced counsellors employ in the therapy room on a regular basis as they've come to understand the universal truths of human experience and emotion and can apply these skills but like the sincere cold reader they do so without recognising that they're doing it, but it still leaves a client in awe of their insight. It's worrying at how easy it is for someone with little or no ethical awareness regarding the potential issues of working with potentially vulnerable adults to gain unconditional trust.

THE POWER OF POSITIVE PREJUDICE

As a trainee counsellor I was always a little nervous about meeting a new client. There were several reasons for this but probably the main reason was that for the first few weeks of seeing clients I was bluffing confidence somewhat. If you meet a fortune teller or medium, you'll find that they come across as so confident that it would seem like an insult to question their authenticity. The clients I worked with had mental health problems, substance misuse and antisocial personality disorder and were coming to me as part of an agreement with a court after some frightening crimes. Mental health patients generally presented low self esteem and automatically accepted me as an expert even though I felt like a fraud. The people who suffered from alcohol dependence came from all walks of life but I would be extremely intimidated if they appeared to have a prestigious job with a good salary. This was because I was sure they would realise that I was a nervous wreck, but instead they automatically accepted me as an expert. People experiencing Antisocial Personality Disorder were hostile to accepting responsibility for their arrest and conviction. Most of them blamed their parents for their upbringing and they blamed their victims for demonstrating a lack of compassion and understanding for contacting the police. I found that as long as I didn't challenge them too much they remained agreeable. I knew that all classes of clients would accept me as an expert for no other reason than they were told I was one, and I walked into the counselling room without any anxiety and felt a lot more satisfied with my performance. After all being a counsellor isn't rocket science, the client does most of the work. But it's true to say that all counsellors feel a little overwhelmed at first and later realise that their work is gratifying as people are seen making changes to their life, and for some odd reason they attribute all their success to the counsellor's own skills.

The counsellor and psychotherapist doesn't need to prove anything to the client as they're already accepted as an expert before the client even meets them. You can't fail with that kind of positive prejudice. As I've already mentioned, my Grandma used to be a member of a club for people with physical disabilities in the seaside town of Whitley Bay in England. Every year they would have a charity fundraising fair and I would agree to do a tarot card stall which proved to be very popular. It struck me that despite being in a room of people buying raffle tickets and cupcakes, how candid people would become when sitting with me at the tarot card table. People employing my services would burst into tears and tell me about their darkest feelings. Others were telling me about marriage problems or their grief at their family moving to Australia. Although these people had voluntarily told me everything that was troubling them I was attributed as giving them this information and they left with total faith in my abilities. Bearing in mind that these tarot sessions were 20 minutes in length it became obvious that these people were affected by something that I would like to bring into the counselling room, if only I could identify what it was. I was obviously doing something that was unconscious but worked a treat. Those who gravitated to the tarot table needed counselling and were looking for guidance or a listening ear to understand their emotional pain. People sometimes just need someone who is unattached to their problems to offload their real feelings as most of them spend an enormous amount of energy in maintaining a façade of someone who is coping. People sometimes present a façade to protect family members from seeing their true suffering. We need someone who'll listen to us and accept what we say without judgement and without involvement. Nothing is more liberating than being given the space to be able to express your suppressed feelings when they've been hidden for a long time, but in order to achieve this in the quickest time possible the practitioner must be able to skillfully evoke trust, faith to enhance positive prejudice. There are people in this world that we automatically trust whether they deserve it or not. People such as doctors, ministers, teachers, and if you're so inclined, fortune tellers will come under that category. All these professionals start with some butterflies the first time they take the role of trusted professional. Counsellors and psychotherapists are among these trusted professionals who are different from the point of view that they work toward stimulating an individual's autonomy and independence and move from unconditional trust in a professional to having a strong sense of self esteem and trust one's own intuition and judgements. If we adopt any skills that a fortune teller uses who is an expert at cold reading then we need to be careful not to make the client dependent upon us for comfort and guidance, that'd be good for revenue but not good for the clients well being. We can see that people who use cold reading have found success in building up a following of people who suffer with deep feelings of bereavement and a sense of meaninglessness. Spiritualist churches in the UK are among the most successful groups who generate a following of people using cold reading. If you get the chance, visit a Spiritualist church and watch the medium throw a generalised random characteristic such as "I am seeing a flat cap and a pint of beer" into a crowd of thirty people in a mining town in the north east of England desperate for a massage from the dead and see what happens. It's fascinating and just a little worrying how susceptible humans are to being manipulated into giving up their ability to grow and mature in favour of being trapped by cults that offer them the opium of pseudo-comfort. Let's not forget that counselling and psychotherapy is a scientifically based therapy and should employ techniques that are scientifically credible, but this is not always what we'll find. I have seen spirituality brought into the counselling room in the form of angel readings, crystal healing and Reiki. Although these techniques are relaxing for clients, it also gives the impression that the therapist has knowledge of psychology and some kind of magic which is presented as credible as scientifically developed psychotherapy. If a therapist truly believes they've spiritual powers, they also have a heightened sense of confidence in what they do and say and become excellent at cold reading due to their confident presence, otherwise known as Charisma. Charisma is a Greek word which means 'gift'. It's used to describe the gift of an attractive or persuasive personality. If someone appears confident and knowledgeable, then they're accepted as being so, after all, who'd feel confident enough to challenge the person who appears to know more than us. Charisma is something that we can generate through our voice, choice of language, body language and gentle propaganda. Propaganda is any form of communication in support of objectives designed to influence the opinions, emotions, attitudes, or behaviour of other people. In the case of the fortune teller you'll find an abundance of propaganda to increase the illusion of credibility. In the UK you can visit popular fortune tellers who claim on their advertising that they're genuine Romany gypsies who are related in some way to Gypsy Rose Lee (whoever that is). You can also find in their waiting rooms an abundance of photographs of fortune tellers standing with celebrities suggesting that they've been endorsed in some way by respected household names like Bob Hope and Billy Connelly. The effect is that before we enter the fortune teller's cinnamon smelling consultation room, we're already impressed by their credentials. In effect we've developed a positive prejudice. This positive prejudice is something that's generated by propaganda and prepares the client to enter the consultation room ready and prepared to accept the authenticity of the fortune-tellers claims. In preparing the mind to accept the fortune teller's credibility, the propaganda has acted as a posthypnotic suggestion. This appeals to the client's strong innate need for comfort and guidance in the same way a child seeks comfort and guidance from a loving parent. The kind of people who suffer the most and have little social support are the most likely to employ the services of someone who offers their inner child love and guidance in a parental role. It's not an unknown phenomenon. Sigmund Freud was the first researcher to identify this process when conducting psychoanalysis with patients. He recognised that the provision of an authority perceived in the therapist results in the client confusing the relationship in the counselling room with a relationship they experienced with another authority figure from the past such as a parent or school teacher, and all the feelings that belonged to that past figure, whether they're love or anger are projected by the client onto the therapist as if they are that individual. This process is unconscious, and the client does not know why they're experiencing such feelings. The process is called transference and results in the client having feelings of extreme love and admiration or fear and hatred for the analyst. There's no doubt that all spiritual practitioners, including cold readers and clergy, enjoy admiration from their followers. Many of these practitioners experience counter transference and enter into unprofessional and emotionally exploitative relationships with clients. The psychologist Carl Rogers was viewed by many of his clients as a grandfather figure and felt nurtured by him in a way that evoked strong feelings of paternal love in his clients. Carl Rogers recognised that his client was experiencing transference and believed that counselling for many clients was the first time they had experienced any form of unconditional acceptance or love. The client's drive to grow as a person without being guided through life by the fear of the withdrawal of love is strong and if the client has been deprived of this type of acceptance, they'll constantly look to others for guidance, discarding their own innate wisdom. The therapist offers unconditional acceptance within professional boundaries, but once the client perceives that this acceptance is unconditional then they form an attachment to the counsellor that could feel like love or dependence. The therapist is trained to recognise this and assist the client to develop trust in their ability to think autonomously and become independent of the therapist. The symbiotic relationship between parent and child is something that's discussed in the subject of Transactional Analysis. According to Transactional Analysis every individual is made up of three aspects of personality called ego states. Jung would probably relate these ego states to his idea of archetypes and complexes. If we fuse transactional analysis and Jung's analytical psychology together, we can see that ego states represent functions and needs. The 'parent' is someone who we are instinctively programmed to trust and follow the instructions of in order to survive and receive love, this will include parents, teachers or any other adult figure that can impart reward or punishment and protect us from potential harm and death. We learn what's acceptable to parent figures and record this information in order to conform to those instructions and continue to receive acceptance and feel safe. The information that the parent ego stores is directly related to how to receive love and affection and is closely related to safety, self esteem, trust, and implicit trust that an adult's instruction is essential to survival. These recordings can be nurturing or critical but either is useful for the child ego to adapt behaviour in order to survive. The 'child ego' is the aspect of personality that reacts to adults. It's the aspect of personality that's feeling and motivation, and it's the child ego that desires acceptance from the parent figure. The child ego will adapt our personality in order to receive affection with passive behaviour in the presence of the parental figures authority. We also have an ego state known as the 'Adult ego' which is rather like a computer. It processes information without the distraction of emotion from the child ego or the bias of the 'parent ego'. The adult ego is the logic we possess and if it acts as our dominant ego state then we can be sure we'll control our thoughts and feelings. It's rare to find someone who has a dominant adult ego. You'll find that the adult ego becomes the executive ego state when taking an exam or when defusing a bomb. In everyday life we change from one ego state to another depending on the circumstance. If we meet a stern looking policeman in his critical parent state while we're urinating in a public place we may become apologetic, passive and emotional. In such circumstances it could be argued that the policeman's parent ego state has hooked our child ego state causing us to feel emotion and adapt our behaviour to the policeman's direction. The 'Parent Ego' can also be nurturing. For example, a teacher may be approached by a young student who has grazed their knee and is crying in their 'child state'. The student is caught in their emotions, stuck in their child state and craves the listening ear of the 'nurturing parent'. it's the 'nurturing parent' that the individual craves when they're in adulthood but feeling emotionally, spiritually lost, or experiencing bereavement. For most adults it is difficult to find someone who'll offer comfort in the same way a parent offers a nurturing environment. To feel safe and accepted as we experience painful emotions is something as a child we can access from a parent figure without any problem, but as an adult it's a lot more difficult to find such nurturing comfort. As an adult we're more likely to be starved of the experience of comfort and acceptance. The result is that we may accept allowing the parasitic person to fulfil that need in exchange for their own gratification. We may accept love and comfort from people who wish to manipulate us. We can see that people use their nurturing parents in order to sell insurance or attract people to their church. The 'nurturing parent' is a great manipulative tool for sucking people into something that's not always in their best interest. This is why the spiritualist churches are so successful, they target those people who are desperate for comfort and use their nurturing parent to hook the child of a suffering soul. We also see that cult leaders can persuade intelligent people to sell their home and donate the money to the cult leader in order to receive his approval. The power of nurturing is probably the most influential tool that a manipulator can use to gain unconditional trust from another individual. This is the main appeal of the successful cold reader whether they use tarot cards, tea leaves, or claim to receive spiritual messages. Of course the same principle applies when someone uses their child ego in order to hook the nurturing parent in order to see the face of a policeman who has stopped you for speeding or persuade the therapist to waive their fee. However I am primarily talking about how the parent ego has been used to hook the adapted child in a client. The opportunity to have our child ego fed with the comfort and attention that it craves is powerful and is the reason we seek and follow a parental ego that appears to be nurturing but could just as well be toxic. Of course, the need to evoke the nurturing parent in another person is more about our innate child egos' need for love. The word love appears unscientific and the stuff of fantasists and romantics, but it's a powerfully captivating human experience which brings with it the need to be loved and cared for and the willingness to do the same for others. This forms an attachment between two people and communities. Without this type of mutual connection we'd find survival difficult. As a child we would die without the love of parents. Our parents would find it difficult to care for their children without the nurturing guidance and assistance of grandparents. And grandparents would find it difficult to live happily without the love, help and attention of their children and grandchildren. Love is essential to our survival and therefore the absence of love may contribute to our death. Carl Rogers believed that love is the primary need of human beings and they'll alter their behaviour to receive it, this would initially be from a parental figure but in adulthood we can still be susceptible to this need if it has not been fulfilled. Without love we would die of neglect, it takes love from the mother to feed and care for her children and it takes love for us to learn that we're valuable as individuals and develop a sense of self-esteem. The counsellor and psychotherapist works in an ambiguous way in regard to ego states. Counselling therapists are in both adult and nurturing parent in the sense they're constantly intellectually and methodically attending to what's being said and recognising patterns as correlations in what's communicated is compiled like a detective while at the same time experiencing empathy and conveying this to the client with warmth and care. The adult state is applied in a nurturing way creating the atmosphere of nurturing parents. This professional approach assists the client to feel safe and have a nurturing space to heal. The ability to create this warm and nurturing environment is down to how the therapist builds trust. When doing cold reading the reader will use the environment to create trust in the same way a therapist will but the difference is that the cold reader is also creating an environment to prepare the client to accept statements that appear to come from the divine. When communicating with a client we're conveying information through our verbal methods using words, tone, volume and speed of speech all contribute toward gaining rapport with the client. If you observe people who are getting along well then you'll find that all these voice qualities match each other and they're synchronised. You'll probably know how uncomfortable it is to have a conversation with someone who talks loud in comparison to yourself; it can be perceived as aggressive. Or if an individual talks quickly where you feel you've got to concentrate in order to keep up with is what's being said it can be distractingly irritating. This means body gestures and stance. The dress and voice qualities of the client need to feel accepted and understood, and one of the greatest things that a counsellor can do is to begin communicating understanding in an open way verbally but also communicate this non-verbally. When I speak of non verbal communication I am including the qualities of voice without words, this includes voice tone, speed and volume. Although these are verbal, they're not words and therefore are included in the way we speak to others' unconscious mind along with orientation, gesture, and posture. There are other forms of nonverbal communication such as pupil dilation and smell, but there aren't many ways to control these functions and farting in the middle of a counselling session will not improve rapport with the client. The client will normally initially phone a therapist before making an appointment. I have found that most clients are at their most authentic at this initial stage because they feel that you cannot see them and therefore have a degree of anonymity. The ego state of the client can be ascertained by the non verbal qualities of their voice. Normally I find that the client will phone my number hoping to find someone who'll patiently and empathically listen and understand. Whether the client is Woody Allen or Darth Vader they'll be ready in their child ego, hoping that they'll find a safe space to be nurtured otherwise they won't bother phoning. When meeting a client for the first time, it's common for a therapist to dress in the middle of the roadway. They'll dress 'casually smart' in order to appear relaxed and put the client at ease. This assists in the client feeling comfortable, but I am not convinced by this view on dress, simply because most of the financially successful counselling therapists that I know are the ones who dress more formally. I know of one therapist who dresses in a tie and jacket and he is the most respected counsellor I know. Dressing in such a way gives an unconscious message to the client that you're educated, successful and an authority in your field. Some people will suggest that such an approach could intimidate a client which could be true, but I'm talking about becoming a counsellor who makes money from their service. These counsellors are the authority in the client's mind before they arrive for therapy because they've no doubt deliberated and given much consideration to whether they believe that the services offered are worth the investment. If they decide to pay a sensible fee, they've already formed a positive prejudice about the abilities of the therapist and are predisposed to accept you as an authority. Fortune tellers are not cheap and charge roughly the same price as the average counselling therapist. It's rare to hear of anyone who has paid a large fee to come back and say that they felt the money wasn't well spent. The positive prejudice that's created by a reasonable fee brings serious and committed clients and also increases our ability to gain trust from them. Of course there are counsellors and psychotherapists who lower their fees or waive their fees for clients who are suffering financial difficulties. But this approach inevitably attracts the needy greedy along with the needy. I used to offer lower priced counselling to those on a low wage but most of the time I would waive the fee because the client would express that they were struggling to pay. The problem for the greedy client who wants a free lunch is that when they begin discussing their life, they can't hide the truth. Counsellors are trained to home in on incongruities and bring them to awareness. I was faced with clients who'd receive free counselling but would within a short period reveal that they were spending silly amounts of money on beer or computer games every week. To find out that you have been duped in this way can be frustrating and also means that the relationship has started with you the therapist being disrespected and devalued in the client's perception. , there's no way to examine a client's finances to ascertain their ability to pay a fee. It's a matter of self respect to charge a fee and have the information to offer to direct them to charities that can offer free counselling if they require it. To have a fee that you're willing to stick to and be prepared to offer the information to acquire free counselling if they need it. Doing this will send the message that you're valuable enough to attract clients who can pay your fees. This may sound unethical to some but if you're to make a sensible income, then you cannot allow your time to be given away without recompense. I always refer clients to free counselling services if they're unable to afford private counselling. This means that we're both taken care of. Unfortunately there are many counsellors and therapists who are attached to displaying the persona of 'nurturing parent' and become exploited as a result. The therapist must remember that when embarking on such a business that the adult ego must be their executive while offering a nurturing environment. If you meet fortune tellers and mediums, they may offer personal readings but this will be at a fee. If you're unable to pay, you'll not get a reading. I spoke to a tarot reader who told me in a shamanic tone that the universe demands an 'exchange of energy.' This sounded great; it's certainly a line I would like to use myself when asked to do therapy for free. It's a great way of moving responsibility for your unwillingness to work for free to the laws of the universe. I like the poetic way that "I charge for my service" was delivered as a spiritual principle that no one could argue with. You'll find many fortune tellers build up a good client base because they're able to have good boundaries with their clients. They're able to provide an environment of nurturing parent with their adult ego being the executive. At all times they're in control. I believe fortune tellers and mediums find balancing the active nurturing parent with the adult ego easy because most of them know they're charlatans and are therefore deliberately misleading clients as to their ability to give a reading. The sincere counsellor and psychotherapist fail to keep their adult ego as executive because they identify too much with their nurturing parent ego and are susceptible to being manipulated by a client's 'adapted child,' in the same way I was when accepting the 'spendthrift' client for free counselling. To attract confidence and success it's important to behave as if your time is too valuable to be given away for free. Positive prejudice is created by many elements, many of which have been discussed already. There are many other ways to create such an effect, but you're probably able to add your own ideas. The magic is in the way you present your approach and maintain professional boundaries. If you look, talk and behave as an expert then this is all the information the client needs to validate their belief formed when they read your advert and you're an expert. It sounds like the technique of con men but I am asserting cold readers contain a lot of conmen whether they're conning other people or are deluded by their own need to believe. But there's another powerful ingredient involved in cold reading and counselling/psychotherapy, which is forgotten about. This is the power of the placebo effect and attribution error.

Attribution error is a process of identifying the effect to an incorrect cause. For example, church members pray over someone who has cancer for several months and their cancer goes into remission. Everyone who has prayed thanks God for his grace and become stronger on their beliefs as a result. The attribution error is that the cause of the remission is not God's intervention, but rather the application of medical science during that period which was successful. Prayer is something that's annoying to the rational mind because it's attributed as being the reason for certain occurrences that are then presented as miracles. For example, a devoted mother needs a computer to help her son with his school work. She prays to God for a computer to come her way. Eventually a friend at work tells her that she was about to throw an old computer out because it was too old and gives it to her. Throwing away computers that have been stored in the house and not been used for several years is a normal thing; there's many people who've forgotten about their old windows millennium computer that's sitting idly in their shed until someone mentions that they need one. But for some reason when this happens God is praised for answering a prayer and faith in the religion is strengthened. The placebo attribution effect is active where there's belief or a certain bias for perceiving certain variables and ignoring others. It's a psychological effect that alters thinking to match expectations. It's a phenomenon that's known to manufacturers of medicines. For example, if a new medicine is created to treat depression, it must be tested by giving a control group a placebo tablet that the participant believes is a new drug but has no medicinal qualities. The researchers can then accurately assess the effects of the drug by comparing its effects to those of the control group. The group that was given the placebo will report that their condition has improved. This effect is extremely powerful and is fuelled by nothing more than the belief in the placebo. The placebo effect can be seen in all holistic therapies such as crystal healing and Reiki. It can also be witnessed in scientifically developed therapies, but is harder to recognise. A good example of the placebo effect is energy drinks. Energy drinks with a mix of caffeine, taurine and sugars are proven scientifically to create an effect similar to adrenaline. This is why caffeine is to be avoided by people who've difficulty sleeping. Caffeine is a powerful drug, it's more like 'anxiety in a bottle' than energy because it mimics adrenaline which would normally become active in the bloodstream when a demand is made upon the body such as exercise or the need to escape from a threat. The odd thing is that people will report that they drink these products to give them an energy boost as if they're going to suddenly wake up and embrace life and feel positive for the rest of the day. The sad fact is that these drinks are more likely to contribute toward panic attacks and negative thinking rather than anything positive. And yet, any feeling of wellbeing that's experienced after drinking one of these beverages is attributed to the drink itself and any suggestion that the good feeling could be caused by the warm sun shining, a tax refund or discovery of five pounds in your pocket will be dismissed as purely incidental. It's daft because anything that simulates energy when you're sitting still relaxing will result in you feeling fidgety, anxious and after some time negative thinking and paranoia will set in. The perceived cure for many is to drink more caffeine, which exacerbates the problem. It's the belief in the drink and the incidental evidence that's used to back up the belief that keeps the individual buying more. It's the same with all the other holistic and alternative therapies. It's rare to hear anyone who uses a holistic practitioner complain that it didn't work, and yet there's no credible evidence that any holistic therapy has any power except to give the client a bit of an emotional boost. Belief is all that's needed in order to create a change in an individual's state of mind. The power of belief upon the mind or placebo effect is powerful for counsellors and psychotherapists. In the same way that holistic therapists gain a successful reputation for nothing more than a misattribution of evidence. But I have to be honest, if I paid £100 for holistic therapy and afterwards felt good because it was a sunny fragrant day I would be damn sure to attribute my feeling of well being to the therapy in order to avoid feeling like a fool. A more sinister placebo attribution error is a cancer patient whose cancer went into remission after her church prayed over her. On hearing the wonderful story of God's grace everyone praises God and grows in faith; while at the same time, completely ignoring the true reason for the remission which was chemotherapy and medical science. Counsellors and psychotherapists use scientifically supported approaches but it cannot be denied the placebo effect is also contributing to success. A good example of this is bereavement. Some people access a counsellor quickly after a loved one dies as a way to take away the emotional pain. Of course grief is a natural process which takes time to complete. There are many stages an individual will have to go through before they can say they feel normal again. The attribution error occurs when the client believes gradually overcoming the loss is 100% down to the skills of the counsellor. The attribution error was made because the client was ready to perceive the improvement in wellbeing from the moment they decided to see a counsellor; in effect they've a bias to perceive things from the point of view of their beliefs. The improvement would've happened whether they had seen a counsellor, priest or Ronald McDonald because humans will naturally adapt to their new circumstances. The counsellor will have an effect if the client fails to adapt over a long period and has additional issues in their relationship with the deceased. The placebo/attribution effect is active and contributes to the success of every cold reader. The counsellor can feel confident even if they've made absolutely no contribution toward the client's improvement they'll be attributed as being the cause by virtue of the fact 's what you were hired to do, and any suggestion that the improvement would have happened anyway would be dismissed or at least minimised. You can't lose with that kind of logic, and yet this is human logic, and this is what makes humans vulnerable to manipulation and exploitation from 'ego and money hungry', holistic therapists and cold readers. The thing that separates counsellors and psychotherapists from these charlatans is that we're guided by scientific research and ethics which are designed to protect the client from exploitation and unnecessary treatments. However, being aware that placebo attribution is a reality which can't be avoided is useful for us to at least trust this process to bring us a greater likelihood of attracting positive feedback or at least avoid negative feedback which is never good for business. The greatest benefit of placebo attribution is that you can afford to feel confident and this will improve your performance as you won't be distracted by self-defeating thoughts that can sometimes creep into mind during counselling.

The ability of cold readers to dazzle people with Barnum statements is fascinating. If people were in any doubt t a cold reader has special powers then the use of Barnum statements will dispel those doubts once and for all. Barnum statements apply to anybody while giving the impression of mind reading. Most clients are usually eager for the cold reader to succeed and will focus their minds to find personal meaning in what the reader presents. In a cold reading, the client believes that the practitioner's accuracy was owing to their supernatural powers and not due to their willingness to cooperate and be deceived. As a rule, clients are compliant whether they're seen by a cold reader, holistic therapist or psychotherapist. The reason for this is that all these therapists have something that the client desires a belief confirming result. Barnum statements are statements that predict a behaviour or feeling that's experienced as personal to an individual. These feelings may never be discussed out in the open with the result that everybody in the world believes their feelings are unique to them. We're all built in the same way and react to stress in the same way, although some people react in bigger ways than others, rather we all have instinctive stress responses that appear during a perceived demand or threat. As humans we also have sexual desires, and a degree of social anxiety in different situations, and we all react badly to change or the threat of change. So demonstrating that you're willing to listen patiently to how the client feels and accurately predict their experience creates a rapport that strengthens the credibility and placebo effect of therapy. We've discussed the use of 'insightful gems' such as fascinating depressed or anxious clients with our ability to understand their situation as well as a psychic by suggesting that they might have difficulty sleeping before they've been mentioned by the client. This insightful gem is accurate because the vast majority of people who suffer depression and neurotic anxiety have issues with sleep, with negative thoughts exacerbating anxiety.

Phineas Taylor Barnum was an American entertainer, circus owner and author. He was excellent in advertising because he understood the principles that attract people to his shows. He was fully aware of the power of propaganda and hype in advertising, but he was also committed to providing value for money to his customers. Barnum despised the fraudulent mediums and spiritualists of his time, because he understood that they were cheating the bereaved out of money and the space to grieve properly for dead loved ones. Barnum even challenged spirit mediums to prove their abilities by offering the incentive of $500, but no one claimed the prize. Modern day illusionist James Randi is offering one million dollars to anyone who can prove that they've supernatural abilities, and no one has managed to claim the prize, and his most famous psychics and mediums avoid James Randi's scrutiny because he is able to expose them by revealing how they've been duping the 'emotionally vulnerable.' Here are some Barnum statements that are commonly used by mediums, psychics, Tarot readers and all other cold readers with surprising success:

List of Barnum Statements:

- Most of the time you are positive and cheerful, but there has been a time in the past when you were upset.
- You are a kind and considerate person, but when somebody does something to break your trust, you feel deep-seated anger.
- I would say that you are mostly shy and quiet, but when the mood strikes you, you can easily become the centre of attention.
- You are sometimes insecure, especially with people

you don't know well.

- You're having problems with a friend or relative.
- You tend to be too critical of yourself
- You have considerable unused capacities that you have not yet turned to your advantage.
- At times you have serious doubts whether you made the right decision or did the right thing.
- Some of your goals are rather unrealistic.
- You have a need for other people to like and admire you.
- You have a generous and giving nature, even though there have been times when you've acted in a rather selfish way.
- I see an initial J. Someone with a J-name is important to you.
- You care most about a few people who are close to you.
- An elderly woman is watching over you in the afterlife.

- You have recently experienced a great loss. (To anyone attending a spiritualist meeting for the first time.)
- You have a lot of unused potential.
- You get a little anxious in new social situations.
- You have sometimes told white lies to save another person's feelings.
- You have been a victim of theft or burglary in the past.
- You have a strong need for approval and recognition.

These are a few of the generalised statements that can be

made by cold readers but I am sure that with time you could think of some more. In 1948, a psychologist conducted an experiment by Bertram R. Forer to ascertain the accuracy of the Barnum statements.

In this experiment the participants were given a list of characteristics. The participants were asked to rate those characteristics from 0 to 10 according to how accurately these statements described them personally. The statements were all Barnum statements. If the theory that Barnum statements is accurate then the score should be high and all participants would possess the characteristics to a high degree.

The questionnaire was as follows:

1. You have a great need for other people to like and admire you.
2. You have a tendency to be critical of yourself.
3. You have a great deal of unused capacity which you have not turned to your advantage.
4. While you have some personality weaknesses, you are generally able to compensate for them. Your sexual adjustment has presented problems for you.
5. Disciplined and self-controlled outside, you tend to be worrisome and insecure inside.
6. At times you have serious doubts as to whether you have made the right

decision or done the right thing.

7. You prefer a certain amount of change and variety and become dissatisfied when hemmed in by restrictions and limitations.

8. You pride yourself as an independent thinker and do not accept others' statements without satisfactory proof. You have found it unwise to be too frank in revealing yourself to others.

9. At times you are extroverted, affable, and sociable, while at other times you are introverted, wary, reserved.

10. Some of your aspirations tend to be pretty unrealistic. Security is one of your major goals in life.

The results were overwhelmingly supportive of the generalised truth of Barnum statements with an average result of 4.26%. We can see from this research that Barnum statements are an effective tool for the cold reader, but to use these statements to increase your own ego or make money misleading people about the fate of dead loved ones. It takes a special kind of evil to create such a delusion deliberately. Using Barnum statements and insightful gems don't just work on the obviously vulnerable and recently bereaved, they can also work on intelligent people who cannot cope with the prospect of their own inevitable death. People are always reminded that one day they'll die and live with this fact, some individuals are rightly disposed to accept any evidence that the supernatural exists and that death is another beginning. We cannot know if there's life after death, or if there's a God, but some people cannot tolerate not knowing. The lack of evidence to support such beliefs suggests that these beliefs are baseless, which makes any reasoning or evidence that presents itself, no matter how small and insignificant, so important that they'll change their entire outlook on life in order to have an absolute belief and comfort regarding their future. Some people will swallow weak reasoning and empty evidence like a child who swallows berries without checking to see if they are poisonous. Spiritual beliefs can be like poison when they include requirements, and this is most probably how most, if not all religions have started throughout the world.

Richard Dawkins compares religion to a virus of the mind or meme, which warps an individual's entire perceptions. The virus is passed on to children and other people through indoctrination and proselytising. Religion keeps its supporters loyal, initially offering love and comfort, and if that doesn't work, they resort to threats of permanent torture in hell or eternal death. Some will even threaten children with excommunication and alienation from their families, which reinforces loyalty throughout life. Social alienation is probably one of the most effective ways to guarantee loyalty from followers, especially if they've been prevented from forming close relationships outside the church. Excommunication for such people means abandonment and loneliness. I have heard some church members describe families who've left the church as dead in God's eyes. Religion and having faith in a spiritual guide such as a medium is rather like eating a piece of meat with a parasite in it. The spiritual guide of a religious organisation will feed off your finances and feed its hungry ego. Religion and spiritual charlatans have existed for thousands of years; it's not surprising that they've developed simple but clever ways to mislead the willing. It's so easy to mislead someone into a belief or faith if they're willing to be misled, and people who visit the cold reader or the church are more than willing, they're eager and desire to be misled. With this kind of mindset it's likely that an individual will accept a cold reader's Barnum statements as absolute proof of the supernatural and proclaim their faith to anyone who'll listen. A common statement from such people is "They told me things that no one could possibly have known."

FISHING.

"She told us things that no one could have known," is a common expression that people who've visited a Cold Reader express. Fishing is where a characteristic or occurrence is suggested with the hope that someone in the audience will accept the message for themselves. For example "Does a flat cap mean anything to anyone?" can result in several raised hands in an audience; this is called a 'hit.' In a large audience fishing is easy; any subject could be suggested, but since we are on the subject of fishing we'll use the example of someone who likes angling.

"I'm seeing a fishing rod. Does a fishing rod mean anything?"

"Ah yes, it's your Tommy. Did he enjoy fishing?"

"Now I'm seeing some sandwiches, does that mean anything to you? What's that love?"

"Oh, you used to make them for him. I thought so, because he's saying he could eat more."

Throwing a random characteristic into a crowd of thirty people can be extremely successful. I once witnessed a medium stand in front of an audience in Northern England and asked "does anyone know of someone who worked in the coal mines and liked their beer?" This produced a few hits, and the medium managed to get the hits down to one person by asking if anyone could understand why onions would be important. Fishing is guaranteed success in large audiences. On a one-to-one basis, fishing may produce much less 'hits,' but this is attributed to the client's inability to make the connection rather than the accuracy of the cold reader. If the client can't make a relevant connection, the cold reader will ask their clients to make the connection after the session, this makes being wrong, the fault of the client. 'Fishing' is something that has no use to the psychological therapist. In group therapy and support groups, asking about negative feelings or delusional thoughts will usually get a 'hit,' because of the genuineness and respect of the facilitator toward the group members, it's known and accepted by everyone in attendance that there are no psychic powers or secret knowledge involved. But if the facilitator wanted to mislead people it would not be too hard to do so. Facilitators of therapy groups need to be extremely careful when expressing beliefs and theories. As a facilitator and counsellor you cannot help but become the projected archetype of the shaman and any expressed personal opinions or spiritual faith will be grasped by some as an absolute truth and made part of their reality.

Pregnant pauses are the gap in a conversation that invites an individual to think or talk. In a one-on-one conversation, most people find these silences extremely uncomfortable and will feel compelled to fill the silence with something relevant. Storytellers, public speakers and comedians use pregnant pauses to offer their audience time to think and digest what has been said before offering the solution to a problem or giving a funny punchline. The principle of 'a vacuum cannot exist' would apply here, because as every counsellor knows, a client cannot tolerate silence for long, and they'll feel compelled to fill it with anything that's relevant and this usually means gleaning useful data that they may have otherwise kept hidden. Policemen also use pregnant pauses when interrogating a suspected criminal, as it's effective, especially when the client is attempting to appear cooperative. Of course a client who seeks counselling does want to be cooperative but they'll have certain defences that are caused by shame and embarrassment which suppress some aspects of their situation. The cold reader also relies on cooperation and pregnancy pauses to draw more information from a client, which increases the perceived success of the spiritual practitioner. The pregnant pause suggests to the client that they're obliged to speak and they feel compelled to speak. It's a powerful tool. A medium, for example, could start fishing for information using pregnant pauses. Giving a piece of information and allowing the client time to make a connection. For example, after giving a client a Barnum statement such as:

Cold reader: "You have an elderly woman watching over you. Does that mean anything to you?

A long 'pregnant pause' will be followed by the client expressing:

Client: "Yes, that's my mum,"

The uncomfortable silence of a pregnant pause causes the client to tell the cold reader exactly who they believe the elderly woman to be, creating the illusion of accuracy to the rightly disposed.

SEEING PATTERNS.

Humans have a tendency to see patterns even if they represent nothing. We learn through a process of pattern matching. We recognise similarities in the things we experience and place them together in our minds to see if there's a relationship or if something new can be created. Pattern matching is something that is so central to our survival in the outside world that it's not recognised as an important part of our inner world. Our inner world, our mind is where we represent reality and experiment in order to understand the world better. Sometimes our pattern matching tendency can lead us in a completely silly direction and result in conspiracy theories that can in some cases be ridiculous beliefs in aliens and assassinations. If we do not have evidence to explain certain events then we might fill the gaps with plausible fiction. Plausible fiction can include any theory or explanation that we apply to a situation to which we do not have the whole explanation. This type of pattern matching has resulted in the complex building of the pyramids and Stonehenge being attributed to aliens and the creation of the universe being attributed to a god. In our mind we store all our concepts of the world including our self concept. In order to maintain mental well being we need to have concepts that agree with each other or we risk becoming confused. We'll be confused because conflicting concepts are a poor guide to the world and will cause confusion and anxiety. Concepts that are in conflict render an individual unsure and anxious when making a decision and so an over dependence on others for decision making and low self esteem can result. 'Homeostasis pattern matching' is a process that humans possess that drives them toward harmonious thought and personal growth through experience. Tea leaves in a cup and clouds in the sky make random patterns that are perceived as pictures. The human tendency to see patterns in things can be fun. Looking at the leaves in an empty tea cup, Dave can see a pattern of the Mona Lisa whereas Julie sees a horse. Both Julie and Dave see a pattern and the same will be true for most humans on the planet. But why do we all want such different things? Our mind is set to perceive things that correspond to a particular interest or need. Dave may be studying art or planning to visit an art gallery, which would explain his readiness to see the Mona Lisa. If he had seen 'The Scream' by Edvard Munch, we could perhaps suggest that he is feeling a bit 'down in the mouth'. Julie may have a passion for horses, perhaps she's always wanted a horse, perhaps it has been suggested that her face is the same as a horse while it munches on a carrot. The true way to find out what the picture means to an individual is to let them talk about it and this is what many cold readers rely upon. When I conducted a small tarot stall at my grannies summer fair, people looked at the tarot cards as I explained their general meaning. I didn't need to use cold reading as the sitter would then take my general meanings in the cards and specify that general meaning to an aspect of their own life. They would look at the pictures in the cards and identify symbols and illustrations that describe their situation either emotionally or symbolically. The sitter or client had in effect volunteered a load of personal information to help me interpret the meaning of the cards. The client was in effect seeing a pattern in the pictures and applying these symbols and pictures to their own life. If the client didn't see a corresponding situation in the pictures, they would identify a feeling instead and it's feelings of anxiety and conflict that usually bring people to a cold reader or a counsellor. The clients were willing to believe and assisted me to interpret the cards to fit their life and left convinced of my ability to see into the unknown. Of course I didn't go to the fair with the intention of attracting the vulnerable or to dupe people into thinking I had powers. I was taken aback when at the end of a reading people wanted to talk about the problems that they believed had been revealed in the reading. They would use the opportunity to tell me how accurate I had been by filling in the wide holes from a general reading with specific information. The clients would spend longer talking about the issues of the reading than the reading itself. The success of the reading was based on the human tendency to seek meaning in all things. Humans need to understand the universe and world we live in and will see patterns in things when there's none there. In the tea leaves we see patterns but it's likely that we'll see something that has meaning to us personally. If you ask a client to look into a tea cup and tell you what they can see and explore what meaning that picture has for them personally then you'll probably find that there's an event desire or emotion connected to that image that's relevant to their own personal reality. The image may also be more symbolic and have archetypal features such as a goddess or a devil. By exploring what the client perceives a great deal of insight can be gleaned that can aid the client to become more self aware and find the clients central problem, unfortunately this cannot be accomplished while we mislead a client regarding our spiritual powers. How do we harness the power of cold reading while at the same time remaining honest with our clients?

THERAPEUTIC COLD READING.

Can the principles of Cold Reading ever be therapeutic? Not if honesty is absent from the relationship. I decided to advertise myself as a Therapeutic Cold Reader to get an idea of how clients would react to tarot readings from someone who is honest regarding their total lack of spiritual power use of cold reading. I know from my experience at Grannies Summer Fair that people are fascinated by the ritualistic and spiritual feel of divination, and so I offered the general public the opportunity to experience tarot readings with a difference. In the advertisement I made it clear that there's no spiritual power involved and that I am a counsellor using an alternative technique to facilitate psychological talking therapy. In this tarot reading I present the cards on the table and discuss with the client what's contained in the pictures. The explanation of the pictures are based on generalities that focus on human needs of love and belonging, emotion and psychological conflicts as well as social insecurities and issues of personal development because these are the reasons that people enter therapy. During the reading the client will nod and make other indications using body language if they find a card relevant to their life. Some clients will offer an explanation during the reading regarding how that card is a good representation of their life and each client will interpret the individual cards according to their own situation, each reading will be unique as it's interpreted and led by the client. After the presentation of cards I ask the client if they're able to relate to any of the cards in the reading. The client is then able to explain in detail using the cards to facilitate their expression of feelings and perspective on their situation. I normally let the reading last for roughly thirty minutes and lead into a sixty minute counselling session. It sounds like a long therapeutic session but the client always feels like it's over too soon and the material covered is overwhelming. Therapists use similar techniques that have the feel of a spiritual ritual but are in fact designed to assist an individual to become more aware of their whole situation in order to gain perspective. The Gestalt therapist uses a variety of shaped stones for the client to arrange in a way that represents their life and family. One stone may represent a career, another stone may represent a family member but it will be how these stones are chosen and how they're placed in an arrangement that assists with insight. A man may place a rough stone representing his mother-in-law next to stones representing his wife and children while placing the stone that represents himself at a distance representing how he feels regarding his relationship status. I have seen stones that represent jobs placed between a man and his family. How a client places the stones can be unconscious but will none the less bring great insight when the counsellor asks the questions. Why did you place this stone here? I noticed you look upset as you placed that stone on the table, what's going through your mind as you do so? There are many techniques that have the appearance and feel of a shamanic archetypal character. They can be used to facilitate counselling and psychotherapy and these all assist the client to come to an insight. For the counsellor it's an honest relationship, where the client is encouraged to become self sufficient and autonomous that creates a therapeutic environment. It's when the client feels the strength to function independently of any intervention that they can truly say they've received something that's therapeutic. Cold readers cannot offer such a service because they work on the principle that the client is dependent on the spirit world for guidance and that guidance can be harnessed through accessing their services. People will always be attracted to the cold reader who offers empty hope and fills their view of the world with fallacy. This is not surprising because as children we learned to unquestionably accept absolute truth from an authority while others are the authority in their own lives. Others remain like children, constantly looking for parental authority to nurture and protect them, and they find this in a church of charismatic ministers, mediums, tarot readers and bible thumpers. Some will find practitioners such as secular teachers, coaches, counsellors and psychotherapists who help them outgrow their infantile need for false comfort and face life's unknowns with a renewed strength and zeal for life. Humans are born with the need for a parental figure because they offer comfort and a sense of safety. Children have evolved to believe everything a parental figure tells them. This is useful, if a child did an experiment to ascertain the truthfulness in the parental rule not to run out into the middle of the road or not to eat toadstools then they would probably have a good chance of an early death. The child accepts beliefs regarding safety, tooth fairy and Santa Clause. Eventually a child is regarded as developing critical thinking and allowed to believe that such fantasies don't exist. Unfortunately the child may spend their entire life believing in God, angels and demons, because their parents do not permit them to stop. The parent personality is both nurturing and domineering and we all develop this aspect in our personality. Our child continues to exist into adulthood and will respond to nurturing and authoritarianism in other people. As an adult we may still have an emotional reaction in some way to an authority figure such as a boss, policeman, minister or general angry person. Both the parent and the child are states of consciousness that exist in all persons. it's the parent consciousness in a cold reader that's attempting to hook the child consciousness in their clients. This will work if the cold reader and the client follow their roles closely. This is a relationship of dependence and inequality, the cold reader is always in a powerful position and the client is reliant upon the cold reader for guidance. For an individual to mature and become free of dependence on a parental figure then the client needs to learn to trust their own judgement and become familiar with their inner shaman. Counsellors and psychotherapists assist a client in getting in touch with their own inner shaman by encouraging recognition of habitual patterns and increasing awareness of personal functioning.

By assisting a client to come to their own conclusions and follow their own inner wisdom they exercise self reliance and autonomy. In a sense they'll become an example of wisdom for other people. In a sense they themselves will become the projected archetype.

Counselling and psychotherapy are viewed as a virtuous and loving profession. It has been compared to the role of a minister who takes the time to care for his parishioners in times of crisis. Many who receive professional counselling have found that it evokes strong feelings toward the therapist of admiration and love; this is because they feel truly valued and accepted in the presence of the Counsellor. The counselling therapist that employs psychotherapy techniques must go through some rigorous training and personal development in order to become ready to embark on such a career. To offer someone an environment of unconditional love resulting in the client's defence mechanisms relaxing so they can feel safe enough to take the opportunity to become more truly who they are, is not as easy as it sounds. We cannot fake a non-judgmental attitude in the same way a politician uses diplomatic skills for the sake of peace. Nor can anyone pretend to have empathy. These qualities are either something that you possess and have developed, or the therapeutic environment does not exist at all. This book will look at the basic principles provided by all counsellors and psychotherapists and match them against the attitudes of some of the most prominent Bible characters. We'll use what Carl Rogers called the "core conditions of empathy, unconditional positive regard and congruence as a fundamental base attitude to counselling therapy and examine if the attitudes we encounter in the Bible are compatible. This book will evoke painful feelings for devoted followers of the Old and New Testament, and I am sure that it will be expressed as anger and indignation. Discussing counselling and psychotherapy in relation to the Bible risks bringing into awareness that the two subjects are not as compatible with each other as many would assume. For Christian counsellors, the reality that deeply cherished spiritual beliefs may have major discrepancies, ambiguities and plain contradictions in relation to values and the morality of a therapeutic outlook may be too much to bear when it comes to awareness. To avoid the anxiety that these incongruities evoke we either need to become blind to them and reason that they're in harmony by using the psychological defence of denial or selectively ignore the values that are revered in the Bible if we do not agree with them. There are many examples in the Bible that shock and upset students of psychological therapies as they become aware that they've embraced inaccurate and incomplete preconceived ideas regarding the virtues of Biblical morality. If you have read this far and haven't slammed the book shut and thrown it across the room in aggressive indignation then you may benefit from at least considering some of the serious issues presented in this book. This book will be painful for the devoted Bible student as it will contain honest observations of what's written. I don't say you have to agree with my suggested interpretation, I am looking at things from the point of view of someone who reads the Bible without a preconception regarding its morality. It's rare that anyone will read the Bible without preconceived ideas. Most people who are born into Christian or Jewish families are told from an early age that the Bible informs our morality and is the purest form of goodness. With this bias in our minds it can come as a shock for many people to find that the Bible also endorses some activities that are condemned by modern societies using the Bible as their moral base. Examining the Bible without bias can lead you to a conclusion about its morality that contradicts its reputation. I do suggest that it would be beneficial to examine your emotional reactions as you read this book. Become aware of the immediate thoughts that accompany your feelings so you can understand the source of your objection or anxiety.

I believe that the Bible is useful for personal development in its entirety when learning counselling and psychotherapy. When we're prepared to identify aspects of the Bible's teaching that are counterproductive to the process as well as identifying helpful examples. Any examples of Bible attitudes that we find uncomfortable can be used to identify areas of our own personal values and beliefs that are in opposition to therapeutic values. This book will focus upon the philosophies of Jesus as a generally positive example and will also make some painful observations regarding the cherished Bible examples and attitudes that are in opposition to the values of counselling and psychotherapy. This book is written from a secular perspective and therefore should not be adopted as theological guide to Christian counselling, but you have probably worked that out for yourself. Much rather, I hope that this book encourages student counsellors to think about their values and resolve any incongruities within their own value and belief system before embarking on offering professional therapy. After all, Carl Rogers viewed incongruities as a sign of neurosis, and we can't become an effective counsellor if we suffer anxiety every time a personal incongruity is brought to awareness in a counselling session. For the purpose of avoiding unexplainable doctrines this book will discuss Jesus and Yahweh (God) as separate entities, and as we discuss their personalities and philosophies, the reason for doing so will become obvious. This book will also take a secular perspective upon the philosophy of Jesus, examining how his examples can be applied to counselling and psychotherapy. We'll also look at other examples in the Bible whose values appear to be in opposition to counselling but are reasoned to be righteous by many Christians. It's important to be able to differentiate between examples that are therapeutic, and which examples have an attitude that's potentially damaging. We'll discuss the more palatable and helpful example of Jesus later, but let's get the part that will be viewed as offensive and the most emotive. We'll now discuss the attitude and philosophy of 'Yahweh', 'God of the universe', in comparison to the values of counselling and psychotherapy.

YAHWEH GOD AND PERSONAL RESPONSIBILITY.

The Bible has 40 writers starting with Moses and ending with John. Most Christians believe that these men were inspired by God to write the Bible making Yahweh God the author of the bible. The Bible says in 2 Timothy 3.16:

"All scripture is inspired by God and is useful for teaching, for reproof, for correction, and for training in righteousness, so that everyone who belongs to God may be proficient, equipped for every good work." NRSV.

When people speak of God they are sometimes talking about Jesus and the loving figure described in the gospels, but we're not talking about Jesus here. We're speaking here about the Old Testament God of Yahweh. The God of the bible introduced himself by name to Moses in Exodus 6:3:

"To Abraham, Isaac and Jacob I appeared as El Shaddai, but I didn't make my name Yahweh known to them." (New Jerusalem Bible)

The Story of the Garden of Eden is where the Bible tells us the Human race begins. From a Biblical perspective, the story of the Garden of Eden and man's fall into sin is key to understanding why Jesus was sacrificed. Apparently this sacrifice was made to pay for the sins committed in the Garden of Eden, and if the story was a myth then Jesus' sacrifice would be meaningless. It's therefore important to examine this story to understand Yahweh's perspective on morality and love. The Bible tells us that Yahweh God created the beautiful Garden of Eden in the Persian area. In that Garden he created man and woman and a tree containing forbidden fruit. They were informed by God that if they ate from the tree that they would be punished with death and as a result they would pass that death on to their children. This punishment meant that they would also be exiled from the garden to become farmers and suffer frustration, illness etc. The consequences of death, alienation from God and a life of futility would obviously be severe in comparison to what they enjoyed in the perfect garden. With the consequence of death being a possibility, any loving parent would protect their children from such an outcome with all their being, but not in God's case. God instead actively planted the poisonous tree in the centre of the Garden and passively allowed a serpent to tempt his children to eat from the tree. But this is not the worst of the situation. When his children ate from the tree, Yahweh then carries out his threat to exile the offending children and allow them to suffer and die as well as passing this punishment onto future generations. It has been said by many devotees in Yahweh's defence that the Tree was a wonderful opportunity for the couple to demonstrate their love and obedience to Yahweh. The question must be asked. What kind of parent would actively and intentionally plant a poisonous tree in their garden, so their children could have an opportunity to demonstrate obedience and love, and allow them to die and suffer? The lack of responsibility that Yahweh demonstrates regarding his role in this situation is alarming. It's comparable to someone who has Munchausen by proxy, where children are intentionally hurt by the parent who should be protecting them. Only someone with a personality disorder would behave in such a way. It's a warped mind that'd think that tempting children with a poisonous tree was an expression of love. If an individual deliberately put a poisonous tree in their garden as a temptation for their children, for no other reason than to give the children an opportunity to demonstrate their love and obedience, then we'd have some serious child protection issues to consider. The explanation that it was the child's fault for not being obedient would probably make the parent seem pathologically irresponsible, and yet people throughout the world accept this excuse as being acceptable. Taking responsibility for our actions is the sign of a mature and well developed individual. To understand our own personal role in events, be they good or bad, is important and the mark of a genuine person. In counselling genuineness/congruence is a quality that something the practitioner must develop through therapy and personal development so that any unconscious motives are in awareness and are dealt with in order to avoid sabotaging the therapeutic relationship. Yahweh's motives in the Garden of Eden are not to provide love and a perfect place for humans to develop but rather it was created as a means for God to gratify himself through the obedience of his creation. Some people have suggested that God gave humans free will to obey or not obey. This is a disingenuous argument when you believe that free will consists of a choice to 'obey and live' or 'disobey and you'll be made to suffer'. Genuineness is a quality where our values and beliefs are in harmony so that we're principally honest with ourselves and are authentic. A counsellor offers a professional love called unconditional positive regard or unconditional acceptance. If we chose to become Counsellors or Psychotherapists for no other reason than to please our parents, friends, church or to attract admiration, then we'd be non-genuine, offering acceptance or professional love on the condition that our ego is gratified in some way, this would not be helpful to the client and potentially damaging. In the Bible the earth is described as being made for man and he had dominion over the animals (Genesis 1:28,29), however God appears to value his people as long as they feed his ego. It could be argued that the whole Garden of Eden story is about God's pathological and obsessive need to be acknowledged and obeyed. God renounces responsibility for the situation by blaming the woman Eve, blaming the man Adam and blaming the serpent who is thought to be Satan the adversary of God (Genesis 3:14-19.)

Ethics of God

Satan does not make too many appearances in the bible. He is blamed for everything that's bad in this world. But the book of Job appears to suggest that Yahweh gave permission to Satan to abuse his most loyal servant for what appears to be nothing more than a bet. (Job 1: 6-12) Satan claims that Job loves Yahweh because he provides for him abundantly. So instead of replying, "who cares what you think, Satan?" he accepts the bet to prove Satan wrong, that God gave Satan permission to kill Job's entire family and livestock and to be left with no social support. Eventually Job is left diseased and longing for death. God allows all this to happen to his most loyal servant to prove that Job loves him unconditionally for no other reason than to keep face. Unfortunately, many children still have a strong attachment to their parents after suffering years of neglect and abuse, so to accept Job's reaction to this kind of behaviour from God as in some way virtuous is highly misguided. Abuse and neglect is wrong, especially if it is carried out with the purpose of feeding the supreme being's ego. The Ten Commandments are said to have been written by God. You would imagine that commands against child abuse and crimes against humanity would be included but they don't even feature. Instead, God makes the first four commandments about building up his ego with the consequence that any deviation be met with execution. I will paraphrase the first for commandments from Deuteronomy 5:1-22

- 1. Don't have any other gods but me, or you'll be executed.
- 2. Do not make any statues and worship them, or you'll be executed.
- 3. Don't misuse my name, or you'll be executed.
- 4. Be like me, and take a day off on the seventh day, or you'll be executed.

These commandments are revered throughout the world, but they're the commandments of someone who is self obsessed, and the consequences for not flattering God by following these irrelevant commands are disproportionate. The Philosopher, David Hume said of Yahweh, *"it's an absurdity to believe that the Deity has human passions and one of the lowest of human passions, a restless appetite for applause"*. It appears that Yahweh is like a spoilt child who takes a tantrum when he is not gratified. Like a domestic abuser, he hurts those he loves by making threats of violence if they make him jealous. Followers of Yahweh, including westernised Christians, have used these commandments to justify, in their own minds, the ethnic cleansing that followed when Moses received the commandments. When he returned to the Israelite tribe he found that many of them were worshiping the golden statue of a calf. This wasn't surprising as they were all from Egypt. The Bible tells us that Moses followed God's command and 3000 people were exterminated as a result of their religious preference (Exodus 32:7-28). To some devotees this would be seen as righteously carrying out God's orders, but in a civilised society where morality is valued and religious diversity is a right, this type of behaviour is nothing more than religious hatred leading to genocide. Any counsellor or psychotherapist who claims to think that this type of behaviour is justified needs to ask themselves why they've made that decision; this type of behaviour is not justifiable in any society that values the diversity of human life. This was the first example of God directing his subjects to commit murder on a mass scale. Before the genocide at Mount Sinai, Genesis tells us that God personally destroyed the cities of Sodom and Gomorrah with no regard for the innocent children who, if the description of the cities is correct were probably suffering terrible abuse (Genisis 19:1-28). Yahweh is also reported to have committed mass indiscriminate genocide when he destroyed most of mankind and animal kind in the flood of Noah (Genesis 6:6-5-8), and whether these events are true is not irrelevant. The fact that these acts of genocide are accepted as righteous by intelligent people is alarming. But this is not where the atrocities end. When the Israelites entered the Promised Land they embarked on a genocidal campaign of ethnic cleansing at God's direction. They were commanded to exterminate all the men, women and children in the most brutal of fashion. In addition to this they were commanded to suspend their natural compassion and empathy by ignoring feelings of regret regarding their actions:

When the Lord your God has delivered them over to you and you have defeated them, then you must destroy them totally. Make no treaty with them, and show them no mercy. (Deuteronomy 7:2).

To have the ability to suspend natural empathy and compassion in such circumstances cannot be accomplished by normal human beings without consequences to their mental health unless they're able to conceptualise and firmly believe that the people being exterminated are vermin. This was the viewpoint of the Nazis during the Second World War when they exterminated as many Jewish men, women and children as they were technologically able. The gas chambers were eventually used as the most efficient way to exterminate great numbers of people. The Nazis started their extermination of the Jewish people using bullets, but this was time consuming and meant that many soldiers who shot the families were left with mental health problems. Many of those soldiers were left suffering from post-traumatic stress disorder and were haunted by a conscience that had been postponed through obedience to a terrifying authority. To ignore your natural empathy in the face of human suffering is a rare characteristic. We live in a world where there's international laws that pursue people who commit crimes against humanity. If there was such a provision in the days of Bible events then you would find Old Testament heroes standing trial for crimes at The Hague. Joshua was commanded to commit the most upsetting of crimes but the interesting point is that he was commanded to do so by Yahweh. Yahweh asks his appointed leaders to use their armies to kill families and to suspend any feelings of compassion or empathy in the same way a Nazi soldier was ordered to kill families.

"So, devour all the peoples whom Yahweh your God puts at your

mercy, show them no pity- " (Deuteronomy 7:16(NJB))

Suspending, ignoring or switching off the natural reaction to empathy is not easy. Certainly people can eventually become desensitised to the suffering of others if they persist and practise doing so in the same way that the employees who work in a slaughterhouse become desensitised to the panic of animals as they realise they're going to be killed. The difficulty is that to become desensitised means that we're no longer sensitive to others feelings or even value them as human beings. People who actively practice killing to become desensitised to the terror and murder of children are in fact destroying their own humanity. This type of attitude is what we see in racist individuals who classify people of another ethnic origin as subhuman or vermin. To dehumanise someone in this way makes it easier for the dictator to encourage killing of adults and children:

Put him under curse of destruction with all that he possesses. Do not spare him, but kill man and woman, babe and suckling, ox and sheep, camel and donkey. (1 Samuel 15:3b (NJB)

All those who are found will be stabbed, and all those captured will fall by the sword, their babies dashed to pieces before their eyes, their houses plundered and their wives raped. (Isaiah 13:15-16)

But it gets much worse. God glorifies acts of killing men women and children but in Numbers 31:17-18 he directs Moses to command that the young virgin girls, which of course would include children of the Midianites, be kept as sex slaves. This is the most sickening verse.

So kill all the male children and kill all the women who have ever slept with a man; but spare the lives of the young girls who have never slept with a man, and keep them for yourselves. (Numbers 31:17-18 (NJB))

For a counsellor who is trained to value and develop empathy and deals with people who've suffered sexual violence, the idea of participating in the implementation of such mass suffering would be unthinkable. Counsellors and psychotherapists would lose credibility if they endorsed the rape of girls who'd watched their families and entire race being slaughtered. It's the most appalling example of ethnic cleansing that has not been exceeded by any war criminal since, and yet some apparently intelligent people become highly anxious and incongruent when presented with this information, and feel motivated to defend the ethnic cleansing of God. Many offer strange reasoning to explain ethnic cleansing, suggesting that this was a 'righteous action'. Excuses such as, 'the nations who were being driven out of the Promised Land were bad and burned their children as sacrifices.' This may sound reasonable to some less intelligent people, but destroying a nation who allegedly sacrifices some of their children to idols doesn't make much moral sense if you're exterminating every child to please God...does it? The Bible appears to suggest that Yahweh has no sense of compassion or empathy. He asked his devoted follower Abraham to satisfy his need for gratification by sacrificing his son Isaac. To take advantage of someone's gullibility in this way is abuse. Of course the Bible tells us that God stopped Abraham from Killing Isaac just before he was about to cut his throat, as if that makes everything alright. It doesn't matter how you like to dress it up; to command anyone to make a human sacrifice as a test of their devotion is rather sick in its methodology. The stress of fighting your own instincts to keep your child alive would be intense. The intervention of God to stop the killing does not excuse the appalling abuse of power that he demonstrated here. Some people justify this action by suggesting that God was also willing to make a sacrifice of his own son to save the human race from the inherited punishment from the Garden of Eden. A God who personally makes a human sacrifice of his own son to appease his own wrath against the human race, whom he himself put in harm's way is a little bit stupid. It's like the psychopath who gave some children some matches and told them not to play with them in the hay barn. When they ignore his instructions and they start to burn to death, he then commands his son to run in the burning barn to save the children while he stands safely outside thinking how grateful the children will be to know that he has sent his son to save them, even though he gave them the matches in the first place. Not just irresponsible and psychopathically narcissistic but also evil. Responsibility is important to counsellors and psychotherapists. If Yahweh was a human and came for counselling how could he be helped to take responsibility? Well it's simple; God does not believe that he has done anything wrong. In fact he views himself as perfect and without blemish. He feels no guilt, empathy, or compassion, and appears to suffer when he is not worshiped exclusively and unconditionally obeyed. He blames everyone for mistakes he has made and expects to be praised for his maladjusted and self-gratifying solution to the problem. So counselling Yahweh would not be possible because he would not turn up for a counselling session unless he was intending to cynically convince a court that he was becoming a reformed character. But because he is the ultimate judge, that'd be somewhat unnecessary.

Autonomy is a quality of independence and self sufficiency. It means that an individual can feel confident about making their own decisions without being controlled by feelings of guilt or the need for affection. You cannot be autonomous if you're motivated to behave or believe in certain things to maintain affection or acceptance from other people. Most people have a degree of autonomy but this is contaminated by their desire for approval from family, friends or a church. This means they're in some way dependent on those entities for preserving a sense of self esteem. Jesus' philosophy was revolutionary in regards to the accepted dogma of the domineering religious leaders of his day, and as a result many Christians ignore the God of the Old Testament and concentrate on Jesus as their leader in effect making him their God. Jesus realised that being genuine and speaking in a moral sense in the face of self-righteous authoritarianism and persecution was the greatest example of freedom and autonomy that a human can provide. This was refreshing to the people who had suffered under the dogmatic restrictions imposed by the scribes, Pharisees and Sadducees. The people of the time were held captive by introjects, bound by deeply ingrained values where feelings of anxiety or low self esteem develop as a result of continuously failing to follow impossible and burdensome rules. Jesus was an example of self determination and of expressing freedom of mind which enabled him to challenge religious leaders. He did this in adulthood and as a child. As an adult he transcended the social taboos of his time by extending acceptance to people who'd be classified as criminals, sexually promiscuous, ceremonially unclean or diseased in the same way a counsellor or psychotherapist accepts people 'warts and all.' He even demonstrated acceptance and caring responsibility toward people who were classified by his culture as apostate or pagan. His story of the Samaritan who comes to the aid of a

Jew who had suffered an attack demonstrates Jesus' attitude of unconditional acceptance of people. The story tells us that the Jewish victim was ignored by his own religious leaders who left him for dead, but the Samaritan who was classified by the Jews as the equivalent of a heretic came to offer aid to the man despite the prejudice between the two cultures. The story had its own moral, but the fact that Jesus used the example of a Samaritan from a positive stance in comparison to his own religion demonstrated that he views all people as having a moral sense without the need for religious affiliation. Jesus viewed all people of all cultures and religions equally and condemned no one, but rather denounced the behaviour of the self-righteous religious leaders who made people's lives more difficult by stimulating guilt and pushing dogma as a means of control. He valued all people as worthy of his time and offered them the opportunity to see a new perspective through his own examples of unconditional love and genuineness. For a counselling therapist, this quality is something that takes time to develop. We all have our own prejudices about different things, it doesn't have to be about race, colour or religion. It can be virtually anything that we've a negative reaction to that's not based on reason. For example, a trainee counsellor discovers that she cannot accept certain male clients who have beards. There's something about beards that makes the trainee counsellor feel angry and suspicious. She used to conclude that her reaction was an indicator that bearded men are in fact dodgy characters. It wasn't until she started studying counselling that she challenged her prejudice and managed to accept bearded men unconditionally. Prejudice can come in many forms and will vary from culture to culture. Women, for example, have historically been devalued by a male-dominated society. Women have greater pressures than men regarding their role in the family and society. In ancient pre-agricultural times a woman's function of giving restricted her ability to take part in the hunting that males in society took for granted. We see some tribes in Africa still live this way. The men hunt for meat while the women stay close to home with the children and gather fruits and roots. This was an arrangement of circumstance rather than of ability, and we know that societies that live that way today have a happy balanced life, where males and females have a great appreciation for each other's role. In time, as the agricultural era started the women were still restricted by their role as a carer to the children but could still contribute by gathering in harvest fruits and milking farmed animals and collecting eggs and of course cooking. But it has never been as easy for women in history to have the same opportunities as men because of the circumstances they were born into. Even though communities are able to assist each other with the care of children it seems that through the millennia that men grew to view women as dependants and women allowed themselves to be dominated because of the sense of dependency. This attitude is acknowledged in Genesis 3:16, and is described as a part of God's curse upon mankind. Women have been dominated by men and still are in certain countries to this day despite the modern growth in human awareness. The prejudice that women experienced based upon the stereotype of dependence is still strong in many cultures. But Jesus was autonomous and didn't devalue women. He had his own viewpoint on how women should be treated and demonstrated respect to the women who weren't in good standing with the community but also the ones who caused embarrassment to the community. When Jesus was invited to Simons the Pharisee's home a woman who is described as leading an immoral life entered the building and began washing Jesus feet with her hair and tears. Jesus saw that she was demonstrating appreciation and shame for her life choice. Jesus probably was willing to consider that her personal circumstances may have led her to making her life choices in order to survive. Jesus didn't reject her despite the prejudice of his host (Luke 7:36-50). His acceptance of women also meant that there were times when they were the first to be given important information. For example, at his resurrection he appeared to Mary Magdalene and other women before he appeared to his male disciples and gave them the privilege of passing the news to the disciples (John28:8-10). This demonstrates that Jesus valued women putting them before men in some circumstances. In fact Jesus also showed compassion to women who broke God's law to access his healing powers *"And a woman was there who had been subject to bleeding for twelve years. When she heard about Jesus, she came up behind him in the crowd and touched his cloak, because she thought, "If I just touch his clothes, I will be healed.""* *Immediately her bleeding stopped and she felt in her body that she was freed from her suffering.. Then the woman, knowing what had happened to her, came and fell at his feet and, trembling with fear, told him the whole truth. He said to her, "Daughter, your faith has healed you. Go in peace and be freed from your suffering."(Mark 5:25-34).* Offering equal respect for women and men is something that counselling therapists take for granted, but prejudice is a devious thought process and can be coloured by our own experience or education that has been generalised. Counselling and psychotherapy is a profession that's still dominated by women. I know that when I was training that in our class I was one of two male students out of fourteen people. The sad result of this is that we become more aware of the abuse that women suffer at the hands of men and here virtually nothing of the abuse that men suffer from women until we begin counselling the general public. I also started to develop this prejudice and started to create reasons in my own mind why this would be. The conclusion I came to was a biological one. Men must be more likely to treat a woman badly because of testosterone. But I was quickly woken up when I started counselling men who had suffered abuse from women. I found that this was equally as common but also as vicious. I was somewhat ashamed of my susceptibility to be influenced by my narrow experience in the classroom and needed to harmonise my viewpoint of the sexes. I could see that both are equal in their ability to show love or hostility and this is probably why Jesus had equal priority to both genders. The difficulty of accepting as a given that one gender has more negative characteristics than the other, then we'll bring that attitude into the counselling room which will impose itself upon the client whether you mean to or not. Our prejudices, or at least our baseless beliefs, are expressed in the most covert ways. We can of course express our attitudes in different ways and there's two ways of doing so that will direct the client to adopt the therapist's beliefs. If a client expresses a thought that implies a momentary hypothesis that the opposite sex is in some way as much as a smile or a not head at the wrong time can reinforce this perspective as a permanent personal reality to the point where the future of relationships are affected. When paraphrasing, a counsellor cannot help including their own frame of reference within that paraphrase. This of course gives the client the ability to correct the counsellors understanding but it can also imply that a certain point of view is correct. This principle can also be applied to racial or religious prejudice. When Jesus entered into the pagan lands he helped a Canaanite woman (Matthew 15:21-28) He also healed the servant of a Roman officer even though the Romans were pagan and an occupying force in the holy land (Matthew 8:5-13). The stress of meeting other people's needs is something that all counsellors suffer from. There are times when a counsellor may be taking on too much work. The stress of carrying someone else's problems in our memory can lead to fatigue and stress. Jesus also suffered from fatigue and desired time alone in order to pray, regain strength and ground himself (Mark 6:30-32). In these verses Jesus *says "Let us go off by ourselves, to a quiet place, to rest a while."* The need to do such a thing reminds us that we must take care of ourselves and that means that during that time we're not available to anyone else. Unless we take that time we'll lose strength and become less effective as a counsellor or psychotherapist. This appears to be common sense but there's many people who in the pursuit of feeding an ego of 'the good person' feel they must experience self sacrifices and suffering to make it valid, this is false and baseless. There's no virtue in suffering, especially if as a result you become less effective as a counsellor and generally anxious. 'Me Time' is important for your well-being and it makes you more effective in all aspects of your life. Jesus may have suffered on the cross, but we do not need to do the same unless the circumstances are serious indeed. An example of needing me time and finding difficulty in getting it is seen by carers of disabled family members. They sacrifice their entire identity to care for a relative, sometimes unable to work and constantly attending to those relative's needs. The need for 'Me time' is important to these people and without it they become exhausted and unable to maintain their well being. Making arrangements to get that personal time is as important as eating food, without it you will weaken. So the example here for counselling therapists is to be aware of your need for rest. It's easy to moderate your time at work when you work independently of an organisation, but when working as a student or working as a volunteer, the temptation to do more than is possible without feeling fatigued is difficult. It's easy to suggest that supervisors are there to assist counsellors and psychotherapists in regulating themselves, but they can't stop a counsellor from overworking or having a work ethic that means they sacrifice their well-being for the good of others. If you read the full account in Mark chapter 6 you can see that Jesus and his disciples were bombarded by people who needed his help and like the voluntary charity counsellor they didn't turn the people away, giving them spiritual insights, physical food, and healing their sick. After this display of self sacrifice Jesus made sure that he took the time that he needed to rest and ground himself (Mark 6:45-47). Counsellors and psychotherapists assist people to become aware of incongruities in their thinking and perspective on life. As we've already discussed, an individual will be happier and experience a greater sense of freedom if they're free of introjects and become authentic and genuine. The mark of a non-genuine person is a big ego with no substance. We see people who wish to project an image of piety and goodness so they can have power over others. We see this kind of attitude in churches where we're continuously disappointed to find that a well respected minister is in fact a child abuser or alcoholic. We also see this in people who want to appear wealthy and successful by dressing in the latest fashions or driving expensive cars, but who are in serious debt to feed this expensive image. There are others who want to maintain an image of love and kindness and become voluntary workers. The great thing about being a voluntary worker is that your employers can stimulate guilt and threaten your self-image if you turn down a request to work. I know of a charity that deals with criminals and hires some paid workers to work on a part time basis (roughly half the week). These same workers are then required to come into work for the rest of the week for free as voluntary workers. In effect these workers are being inauthentic as they're not doing the work for the good of their clients or the charity but rather maintaining a self image of care to secure their job. In a sense the charity is run by non-genuine people who use guilt to control their staff while at the same time the staff are non-genuine because they pretend to be committed to the work to secure their position. The inauthentic individual builds a façade or falseness to protect their ego. Being non-genuine or inauthentic is something that Jesus was clear to condemn and his main target for exposing. In counselling and psychotherapy, the client is helped to become more genuine by exploring incongruities. If they express that they love their work but at the same time provide an abundance of proof that most of the different aspects of work are hated then it could be that the client is being inauthentic. Some people do love their workplace and their position especially if they get a promotion to management. However if they hate the work in a management position and desire to go back to their previous position then they would be inauthentic to continue thinking that they love their job, instead they would be more accurate to say that they love their prestigious position and the money that it brings, but hate the work itself. Jesus recognised the power of a façade when he accused the teachers of the law of being inauthentic.

"Woe to you, teachers of the law and Pharisees, you hypocrites! You are like whitewashed tombs, which look beautiful on the outside but on the inside are full of dead men's bones and everything unclean. (Matthew 23:27 NIV)

Jesus appealed to everyone's sense of responsibility. He assisted the extortionist of his day to at least think about the effect of their actions upon the poor people. Jesus didn't do this by condemning them, but rather by befriending them and bringing to their awareness their own natural sense of compassion (Luke 19:1-9). It can be difficult to work with criminals. As counsellors we're trained to have a heightened sense of compassion and empathy and to allow the suffering of someone would be difficult to understand. To hear a story from a man regarding how he mugged an old lady and left her afraid to leave the house again, or to hear how a paid carer stole from the purse of a pensioner that they were caring for is difficult for any counsellor especially if the client is more upset at how the crime has affected their liberty rather than the victim. I have counselled violent criminals and was suppressed to find that there was no sense of guilt regarding their crimes or any kind of compassion for their victims at all. There was a sense of pride from some of them as they described their crime; their only regret was getting caught. In Zacchaeus' case he demonstrated his change of heart and responsibility and compassion by giving half his positions to the poor. The desire to take responsibility for his crimes in some way justified Jesus intervention, but unless a convicted criminal expresses some desire to take responsibility for what they've done, they're probably wasting your time and will stop attending their sessions as soon as the court reduces their sentence because they've used you to give the illusion of responsibility. I even heard of a woman who beat her children viciously and as a result the police and social services intervened. She immediately started to receive counselling and appeared to be taking responsibility, using the faces of the authorities until it transpired that she was receiving counselling for generalised anxiety and the counsellor was unaware that there were any anger issues or child protection issues. Counsellors need to be aware that we can be used by criminals and that Carl Rogers' assertion that "people are essentially good" is not scientifically credible. Judas was an example of evil. He allowed the arrest of his friend Jesus for money (Matthew 26:14-16).

LOVE: THE PRIMARY NEED

The need for love is an instinct which Carl Rogers believed is the primary need of humans. it's true that humans need food and shelter but a child will suffer and die without someone who loves them enough to provide those things. If an infant is rejected by its mother it will not be fed and will die without altruistic intervention. It's comforting to see that altruism is an instinctual facet of humans and other mammals in the animal kingdom. A child whose family has died will usually be adopted by another family who naturally feel compassion and a compulsion to react to the child's needs. Elephants have been observed with the same behaviour and they're susceptible to adopting a calf who has become lost from its own group. We all have a love instinct which protects us and forms the basis of our successful communities and has contributed to our survival as a species. To be accepted unconditionally is a truly wonderful experience. It requires nothing from us in return as is demonstrated by a mother who cares for a demanding baby when she is tired and wants to sleep. A father who visits his son in prison after he has committed serious crimes demonstrates it although he may suffer pain as he does so. Unconditional love is something that has no rules in order to maintain, it requires no payment or reciprocal feelings of affection. This does not mean that we accept the actions of people as acceptable, rather we accept the person in the same way Jesus did, without condemnation. Jesus accepted people who weren't only condemned by society but also were seen as somewhat of an embarrassment. For example, in the company of well respected people, he wasn't ashamed to demonstrate that he valued people when he showed warmth to such people as prostitutes and adulteress who'd normally be stoned to death. He accepted Lepers' who were classified as ceremonially unclean and avoided, also accepted people who were seriously mentally ill or classified as Pagan. The difference between 'unconditional love' and 'conditional love' is the difference between being controlled by society or family and personal autonomy. It's difficult to get the balance right as our need for love is said to be at the heart of our behaviour and thinking. Rogers believed that the need for love is so strong that humans will adjust their behaviour to social requirements in order to receive it in whatever form it's offered whether it's conditional or unconditional. The power of counselling and psychotherapy is found in the gradual growth awareness in the individual as they become conscious of their introjects and see how they've held them captive their whole life. This is important as the person who experiences autonomy has enough free will to make a responsible decision. Jesus says in

"And you shall know the truth, and the truth shall make you free." (John 8.32)

This statement has been given many interpretations but the idea of freedom is forgotten when discussing this passage. It's the opposite of being in captivity, which is exactly what people are if they allow themselves to be blindly controlled by the rules of others. Freedom is the position of a truly autonomous and independent individual. Jesus was such an individual and encouraged the same qualities in others. He spoke the truth of how he saw it and effectively argued against the introjects that had been passed down from generation to generation, which suppressed free thinking and encouraged conformity through fear of God's rejection. Freedom is a possession of all people but we're constantly reminded that there are consequences to acting on freedom. We're told that expressing our autonomy can result in alienation from God, our families or a religious community or being imprisoned by the state. To become ostracised from the people that we desire to receive love and acceptance from can have tremendously negative effects upon our ability to develop self-esteem. Any deviation from the accepted dogma of the majority can result in serious physical experiences of guilt and anxiety. This guilt and anxiety is the fear of abandonment and death. This is not surprising as abandonment as a child would surely result in death as we could not care for ourselves, and without the support of our families in old age or when suffering sickness we're sure to be more likely to deteriorate and die sooner than if we had their support. Losing a sense of God's acceptance for many can result in a feeling of hopelessness for many in times of distress, so we can understand the power of conformity in the face of such powerful consequences. As we can see conditional love has a strong bullying influence upon its victims who may feel that they would like to behave or think autonomously but choose to conform in order to maintain any sort of acceptance or love.

"If any individual refuses to obey what we say in this epistle, you must mark that man, and have nothing to do with him with the purpose that he becomes ashamed of himself" 2 Thessalonians 3:14

To actively make somebody feel ashamed is to actively impose upon your own valuing system. This valuing system is known in counselling as conditions of worth. Conditions of worth are the means of measuring our value against introjected rules. It's difficult to live in a community where rules of conduct do not exist as this would result in anarchy, but conditions of worth are not about our relationship to society although some societies have strong conditions of worth as part of their religious culture, rather they're the introjected commands that we've assimilated from specific people to gauge our value and worthiness of love. Being free and independent may appear to be without any benefit if we live in a community where conditions of worth are prevalent and ostracism is the consequence. As a result many sacrifice their freedom in exchange for the captivity that conditional love provides. We learn through life how to be accepted by our parents, peers and teachers by learning to conform to conditions of worth. We record this into our minds as a guide to behaviour and feel guilt and low self worth if we fail to live up to these conditions. These introjects exist as an exact recording of our past that we've adopted as dogmatic truth without testing its credibility against reality.   As children we're bombarded by rules and regulations that are usually sensible and designed to keep us safe. No one would disagree that it would be wrong not to give guidance to a child regarding road safety. This doesn't mean that the parent has withdrawn love from the child but rather that the parent is reinforcing love by protecting them from a factual danger, which would be fatal to test against reality. Children are not always given guidance regarding what's good for them but rather sometimes they're commanded, manipulated and coerced to conform to parental preferences and social/ cultural norms which preserve the ego of the law giver. The example of the university lecturer who wants his son to go to university to study law is an example of this. If the son goes to university to study law then the father can feel validated and proud to express that his son has inherited his intelligence. The problem for his son is that as a child he expresses that he wishes to pursue the career of an actor or dancer. The father, upon seeing any desire to pursue an opposing choice of career, experiences stress and panic, he may also express this as anger. As a tactic, to alter the child's choices or desires, the father may attempt to remove love and warmth as a manipulative tactic until the child conforms to his father's conditions for receiving love. The father may take this tactic to the next level and combine his withdrawal of love with anger, threats and intimidation. We see this type of attitude when a child is physically harmed, yelled at or told they'll be written out of their will. All of these tactics are extremely effective in controlling the life course of a child as it causes panic. Panic stops our intelligent brain from working and makes us revert to our innate and learned responses. The result is that we're unable to examine the information we are subjected to absorbing them without evaluation as a dogmatic introject. Jesus didn't take such an attitude, he allowed people to choose their own path and take responsibility for the consequences although he was always ready to offer his insight on the situation with stark honesty (Luke 22:34). To allow someone to take their own course after you have expressed an objection or concerns is an expression of unconditional love. To still accept an individual after they've caused offence is also an expression of unconditional love (Matt 5:39). By receiving unconditional love we no longer need to conform to the requirements of others and can more easily become genuine and authentic. Unconditional love is something that's difficult to imagine as being used as a tool in the counselling room. It's not something we can bring our bag in the same way a doctor would bring out a stethoscope. Unconditional love is something that you either are able to express because it's part of your personality or you'll need to develop it through experiencing therapy and personal development. Most students are astounded to find that the kind of love that they offer to people is conditional and struggle to accept that they need to nurture that aspect of themselves. Some followers of Christianity who pride themselves on their ability to feel and express love are upset or attempt to reason on their devotion to conditional love. Many will reason that they put conditions on expressing love as an expression of unconditional love in order to save the individual from the wrath of God. This attitude shifts the responsibility for manipulative behaviour on to God rather than being honest and saying I require this behaviour from you and attribute my requirements as coming from God, "Conform to MY conditions of worth and make me feel validated." This was an attitude that Paul would advocate but not one that Jesus would support. Paul created new laws and values that didn't come from Jesus or God. Obedience to Paul's new laws would bring favour from no one but Paul himself. For example, we've already seen the respect and dignity that Jesus afforded women. However, Paul placed women in subjection to men. *"Women should remain silent in the churches. They're not allowed to speak, but must be in submission, as the law says." (1 Corinthians 14:34)* Notice who is making the commandment in the next verse regarding women. Is it Jesus, God or the apostle Paul? "A woman should learn in quietness and full submission. *'I' do not permit a woman to teach or to have authority over a man; she must be silent. (1 Timothy 1:11-12)* Notice that the Apostle Paul states "I do not permit" rather than "God does not permit" or "Jesus does not permit" or the "apostles of God have decided." Paul makes this commandment something that's based on his own authority. In this way he elevates himself in a way that has never been done in the Bible sense Moses took the credit for making water appear from a rock for instead of attributing the miracle to Yahweh, (Numbers 20:12). The difficulty of making his own rules is people must conform to them in order to be accepted by the church. It's difficult to discuss a word like love with so many different meanings to so many different people and still keep scientific credibility. The term unconditional love in a scientific setting where research has established its validity needs to be given a term that separates it from its conditional counterpart. Carl Rogers renamed Unconditional Love as Unconditional Positive Regard or Acceptance to assist people to prevent misunderstanding regarding its true meaning. In counselling, Unconditional Love can be used as a tool in an environment where the client's authenticity is allowed to flourish and is something that the counsellor or psychotherapist provides through their attitude of unconditional positive regard. For many who employ such services, the experience can become overwhelming as they begin to speak the genuine truth as they experience it, and begin to come to an awareness of feelings and desires that have been suppressed throughout life. They can experience unconditional love for themselves and other people in their lives. *"Jesus answered, "Everyone who drinks this water will be thirsty again, but whoever drinks the water I give them will never thirst. Indeed, the water I give them will become in them a spring of water welling up to eternal life." (John 4:13-14)* Accepting oneself unconditionally does not mean that an individual has become vain or without conscience. Conscience is much a part of a normal human being, only the psychopath lives without conscience. This being true, then we'll love and accept ourselves in the sense that we have greater self esteem. Instead of judging self based on introjects from parents and significant others the individual is increasingly able to trust their own ability to evaluate truth. The ability to evaluate situations, people and self without inhibition is the quality of having an internal locus of evaluation, meaning that we're motivated by trusting our own logic or intuition. This can be a problem for some who believe that all morality must come from their God or their minister's interpretation of scripture. Jesus demonstrated that this obedient attitude wasn't an attitude that he approved of and he provided an example of an internal locus of evaluation for us to follow in the way he expressed his freedom to speak the truth as he saw it. He concentrated on raising the people's self esteem by offering unconditional positive regard which was demonstrated when people failed to follow his requests. Mattew 9 states: '*and their sight was restored. Jesus warned them sternly, "See that no one knows about this." 31 But they went out and spread the news about him all over that region.('Matthew 9:27-31)* he didn't condemn those people who either ignored his requests or disappointed him. But rather he still accepted them and expressed unconditional positive regard.

Absolute truth is not something that humans have the ability to experience. Our perception of experiences is always affected by our past and our current state of mind. There are so many variables that can affect our perceptions and consequent beliefs that it's impossible to attribute our beliefs to anything that could be described as absolute truth. The claim is made that people know the truth, but people who believe they have the truth there's also as many interpretations of that truth especially when it comes from scripture.   For every person on the planet we can claim to have our own personal perception of the truth, or more accurately, we can only experience and interpret reality from our own frame of reference. Our frame of reference is so influenced by past recordings, personal biases and current mood that no one person could lay claim to knowing absolute truth, and it would be arrogant to make such a claim. For many people the idea that some people may have different perceptions of reality to themselves is too much to bear and they embark on differing methods of changing the mind of an opposing viewpoint. This type of attitude is about conditioning an individual to introject your beliefs so that you can feel validated but this runs the risk of filling the listener with conditions of worth if they're dependent upon you for love or acceptance into a religious community. This can have devastating effects on people who have complete faith in friends, parents or ministers who withhold love and acceptance until their viewpoint has been accepted. Paul gave good advice in this regard to assist an individual understand the value and limits of truth:

Prove all things; hold fast that which is good. (1 Thessalonians 5:21)

When we prove things we're not employing intuition or

listening to someone who we believe is trustworthy. To prove things means we must test things empirically and be open to the possibility that our conclusions may have inaccuracies that can be refined by further experience. This is the type of approach that a scientist takes toward reality. Scientists are always open to updating their understanding of truth as new information presents itself and can with confidence express that they've 'proved all things.' George Kelly took the view that we construct a complicated array of mental formations which represent our reality. He asserted that constructs weren't static but could be disassembled by experience and rebuilt based on more accurate information. Viewing reality as constructs makes us less dogmatic and less susceptible to introjects as they also exist as constructs that can be tested against reality. In counselling it's important for the therapist to take this hypothetical approach to truth, realising that as a therapist we enter the therapy room with our own set of experiences and beliefs that will represent our own truth. Being non-dogmatic about our personal truth makes us more open to understanding the truth of the client. To be able to do so opens the door for empathy. Personal Truth is something that people who are held captive to conditions of worth cannot experience until they become aware of their introjects and learn to accept their own natural feelings, perceptions and meanings without the internal voice of chastisement dulling the experience. Being open to experience in this way allows an individual to become more authentic rather than being like a robot who functions on the programs that have been uploaded by an operator who needs you to function in a certain way so that they feel validated in some way. The difficulty of allowing ourselves to be a robot is that we never become autonomous and in turn cannot feel validated as a human being. Having a sense of value as an autonomous human being is essential for a happy existence. It means we can be responsible for all aspects of our being. This is someone who feels the liberating authenticity of experiential truth. Experiential truth is the truth of the moment, which is open to change as it's experienced through the senses and is genuine in the sense that it's not affected by introjects but is owned by the individual as their own reality and their own wisdom.

It must be stressed that not all of the New Testament characters had the attitude of Jesus, in many ways the attitude that's presented is a mixture of the attitude of Jesus and the attitude of Yahweh. This mixture appears to have altered the perception of what's acceptable from a New Testament point of view. This is perhaps because the apostle Paul, who was a deeply religious Pharisee in his past, was well educated in the attitude of Yahweh. This attitude would have affected his understanding of Jesus' teaching and he may have experienced incongruence between the contrasting perspectives. His solution was to avoid quoting Jesus in his writings and instead present a moderate law where death wasn't the consequence of deviation. Paul's own words could be used to describe the effect of his teaching:

Your glorying is not good. Know ye not that a little leaven, leavens the whole lump? (1 Corinthians 5:6)

This means that a small change to teaching will alter its message as it must be seen holistically and apparent ambiguities harmonised for it to be credible and accepted. Paul was the most influential missionary who wrote most of the New Testament and it's his influence that has created the organisation of the modern churches today. It would be useful to be aware of the pitfalls of employing an attitude that's accepted as righteous by a church but is in opposition to the principles of counselling therapy. Such an attitude is in opposition to the principles of therapeutic counselling but may also be against the philosophy of Jesus.

Jesus said to them, *"Watch and beware of the leaven of the Pharisees and Sadducees." (Matt16:6)*

Paul is celebrated as the founder of the Christian church in the west but he also appeared judgemental and rejecting of people who do not fit his ideals and as a result would be an unsuitable example for a therapeutic approach. However, the apostle Paul can be used as an example of how some dogmatic forms of morality can nullify a counsellor's ability to offer a therapeutic environment and potentially cause damage when they fail to apply the liberal principles expressed by Jesus. Paul's letters take time to reject and condemn people in a way that would make it difficult to reconcile to the philosophy of Jesus. (Matthew 12: 20). For example, Paul took time in his letters to criticise the other apostles in a way that publicly raised himself above them in the same way a politician criticises a rival to elevate his own position (Galatians 2: 1-14 2-Corinthians 11: 5-60, 22-33). He rejected people based on sexual orientation, classing them as fornicators (1 Corinthians 6:9). For a counsellor or psychotherapist to view a Homosexual person as immoral would disqualify them from working with such people. Most regulatory registers will not offer membership to anyone who discriminates based on sexual orientation. As we've discussed, Paul also used his power to suppress women in a way that would be difficult to reconcile to the principles of counselling therapy. All of these attitudes expressed by Paul would invalidate anyone's ability to become a counsellor, especially if they hide behind the façade of piety. This type of attitude also emulates the attitude of the religious leaders of the time that Jesus criticised as suppressive toward the people which isn't surprising since Paul was originally a Pharisee (Matthew 23:4). An effective counsellor is prepared to accept any individual who enters into the therapy room without judgment or prejudice. People generally don't walk into a therapy room unless they're suffering in some way. Their suffering may be as a result of negative events, relationship difficulties, spiritual or existential problems and soon and the last thing they need is condemnation or a counsellor who attributes their suffering to sin. Most people who suffer and access a counsellor demonstrate responsibility in tackling problems. There are other times when counsellors are employed by criminals in an attempt to take advantage of counsellors' positive outlook on human nature and manipulate the justice system and other authorities so that they'll attain the guise of responsibility. This is done in the hope that they'll gain leniency in the courtroom, but this is rare and when it does happen it's a short-lived affair when their cries of "I victimise because I am a victim!," is challenged with intelligent logic. Judas, for example, was a compulsive criminal. He could be compared to what we'd call days as a psychopath. He took money in exchange for his friend's life and only felt regret when he was exposed. People realised that his righteous exterior was nothing more than a façade. He even attempted to show responsibility by handing the blood money back to his employers who contracted him to deliver his friend into their hands. His regret was nothing more than sorrow for his lost reputation as it was for so many sociopathic criminals. Many criminals will pursue counselling to give the impression of taking responsibility but I have found that their commitment to self exploration usually stops as soon as it's no longer useful to their courtroom defence.

Most people are not like this and will enter the counselling room with the need for your acceptance and the need to bring balance to their thoughts. These people need an environment of unconditional acceptance where there's a non judgmental counsellor who can put judgment to one side in order to experience empathy with the client, and also the counsellor must be genuine, in other words not putting up a façade of acceptance while secretly viewing the client as a sinner. Jesus was motivated to help such people in distress and would show compassion in a way that brought criticism from the religious leaders of the time. His unconditional acceptance of other people meant that he could defend his actions undeterred by religious or social introjects because he also had unconditional acceptance of himself. His fairness and plain common sense approach to protecting people's welfare resulted in his persecution and death, but when he died he did so as a man with the freedom to think and act as an individual. The unconditional self-acceptance that Jesus possessed meant that he could as a child challenge educated men in the temple and, as an adult, openly criticise the self-righteous actions of religious leaders of his time. Self-esteem can develop when we experience an environment where unconditional love is experienced from family or friends. This type of environment is rare, and especially difficult to maintain in a conservative-religious family environment that imposes its rule in the same way that the Scribes and Pharisees did if it's not balanced with the perspective of Jesus. Jesus is loved and admired by people throughout the world because he offers them something fundamental to our wellbeing and continued personal growth, he offered us his example. The Bible is a beautiful piece of literature but it's ambiguous in its values. The discerning reader can decide whether it's in harmony with counselling and psychotherapy. I believe that generally it's not. Even though Jesus left us a positive example we find the bible itself is dominated by an attitude of intolerance, ethnic cleansing, and genocide for the purpose of gaining love from an egotistic God. To follow Yahweh is in my opinion to reject the values of counselling and psychotherapy.

I am sure the subject and the disrespect I appear to have toward God will annoy many people. I have to admit I also have disrespect toward Darth Vader and the Wicked Witch of the West, but there's nothing stirs emotions more than disbelief in the Biblical God. He is the uncontested champion of 'evil character's' fiction he has produced to date. I wanted to discuss Friedrich Nietzsche, Jean-Paul Sartre about bad faith and existentialism, but it probably wouldn't have added too much to the points being made. I also wanted to Discuss Viktor Frankl's logotherapy and his discussions on the Man's Search For meaning, but these are people you can research for yourself if you're interested

In the meantime, please contact me and let me know what you think of this book. I am always happy to receive constructive feedback and criticisms I can put right.

plesseycastle@outlook.com

I hope you found this book as ranty as I did.

All the best and thanks for taking the time to read.

Alex H Parker

9 79 8 6 7 4 0 0 4 4 2 4